WOMEN'S OCCUPATIONAL MOBILITY

Women's Occupational Mobility

A Lifetime Perspective

Shirley Dex
Lecturer in Economics
University of Keele

St. Martin's Press   New York

First published in the United States of America in 1987

Printed in Hong Kong

ISBN 0–312–88789–2

Library of Congress Cataloging-in-Publication Data
Dex, Shirley.
Women's occupational mobility.
Bibliography: p.
Includes index.
1. Women—Employment.   2. Occupational mobility.
I. Title.
HD6053.D49   1986   331.4′1272   86–13727
ISBN 0–312–88789–2

To my mother, Alice Dex

Contents

List of Tables and Figures

TABLES

FIGURES

Acknowledgements

The research described in this book was originally part of a project funded by the Department of Employment. The views expressed here are the author's and they do not necessarily reflect those of the Department. I would like to thank the staff of the Department of Employment and the Office of Population Censuses and Surveys who provided help and advice in the course of this research. I am particularly indebted to Ceridwen Roberts, Jean Martin and Heather Joshi for their help, encouragement and inspiration. Thanks are also due to Paul Collis of the Keele Computer Centre, Kim Pickerill who produced the typescript and to the Department of Economics and other colleagues at Keele.

SHIRLEY DEX

1 Introduction

If women were thought to have careers at all, they used to be thought to have a career only, or rather merely, as mothers. The vast increase in women's employment over the post-Second World War period has led to a recognition that women might have employment careers. The tendency to think that a woman's main role is as a mother, working at domestic tasks has meant that very few women were considered to have employment careers as such. The term 'career woman' was used to describe these few, who were thought mainly to be single and in professional occupations or possibly some sort of freak. These conceptualisations of women's employment histories have come under attack from two sources; women can be seen to be spending more of their lives in employment; the notion of a career which underlies the earlier views of employment histories has also been heavily criticised since it is thought to be unduly restrictive as a description of both women's and men's experiences. The tendency to view domestic tasks as inferior to employment has also been challenged and the counter-proposal which suggests we should see unwaged work as a fully-fledged occupation, has been advocated.

This book presents the results of an analysis of a new source of information about women's employment over their lifetime, the Women and Employment Survey. The analysis is set in the context of the debates about the nature of 'careers' as such, and this issue is vitally relevant to other debates in sociological theory and labour market analysis. These results allow a foundation to be provided for an appropriate set of women's careers based on their empirical employment histories; a foundation which has previously been lacking. The analysis starts off with a more basic question therefore: How do women move between jobs over their lifetime? This book revolves around this central question.

The facts about women's mobility between jobs over their lifetime have been recognised as being important both to policy-makers and to the academic community. These groups both recognise that women's occupations are central to their unequal status and prospects in comparison with men. Occupations more generally are of central importance to the lifetime rewards received from employment and the standard of living which ensues. An understanding of women's segregation in a small number of occupations is therefore recognised as being crucial. Some steps in this direction have been made through clarifications of the notion of occupational segregation, and from the recognition that many women's primary responsibility for child rearing involves a loss of occupational status as well as a loss of work experience. The statutory provision of maternity leave has been a development which helps to protect women's occupational status across childbirth but the take-up of maternity leave appears to be linked to women's initial occupations; we return again therefore to the importance of women's occupations. Information about women's occupations and their lifetime movement between occupations is also required to resolve academic debates about women's role in class analysis; about theories of the operation of labour markets, and for understanding changes in the industrial structure.

We have known for some time that women are segregated into a small number of occupations (Hakim, 1979), and that their lower earnings than men are in large part attributable to this occupational distribution, rather than to women being paid a different rate than men for doing the same job (Chiplin and Sloane, 1974, 1982). It is also clear that women's employment experiences are related to divisions of labour within households between gender groups. Sources of cross-sectional data have been available to document these relationships. The issues which have not been examined are those which relied upon sources of longitudinal data showing experiences over time, since such data have been unavailable. We have not been able to determine, therefore, whether women are segregated into the same occupations over their lifetime; whether they have identifiable patterns of occupational experience over time; whether they experience downward occupational mobility only, or mainly, at childbirth; whether they have strategies of occupational choice over time through which they can combine employment and domestic responsibilities. We also know relatively little about how the industries of women's employment fit into the structure of employment opportunities and changes in that structure in Britain. These questions are addressed in the chapters which follow.

Information about women's employment histories, which is necessary to begin to answer these questions, became available through the Women and Employment Survey (WES) carried out by the Department of Employment and Office of Population Censuses and Surveys in 1980. A summary of the survey is provided in Appendix 1. Prior to this survey, small scale empirical research had collected information of women's employment histories (Chaney, 1981, Yeandle, 1984) and large-scale surveys had collected employment history data over a limited life span (Elias and Main, 1982; Stewart and Greenhalgh, 1984).[1] The WES survey was the first systematic large scale recording of women's employment histories over their whole life up to the interview in 1980. It contained the employment histories of 5320 women between the ages of 16 and 59 in 1980. Its availability meant that the experiences of a nationally-representative sample of British women could then be documented. The fact that the women were of varying ages meant that varying amounts of information were available for the women, and problems of analysis were raised by this fact. This large-scale survey provided an opportunity for a unique analysis, nonetheless, and what it lacks in detail, because it was so large, it makes up for in being systematic and representative. Fortunately, we also have smaller scale studies which have documented, and will go on to investigate further the more subjective and discursive information about women's employment histories which such a large scale survey was unable to tackle.

This book describes the types of employment histories of British women; in particular their patterns of occupational mobility over a lifetime. Other aspects of women's employment histories have been written up elsewhere (Dex, 1984). It is highly appropriate to an understanding of women's working lives that this lifetime perspective be adopted, although a whole set of issues of method and technique are raised by these data.[2]

It is only through such a lifetime perspective that more of the integral relationships between women's work in the home and in the market place become visible. The variation in women's employment over their lifecycle is one way in which women's varied responsibilities and the extent and importance of the sexual division of labour become evident. This book concentrates on the employment side of women's experiences although it is obvious that women's experiences, responsibilities and relationships within households are always intruding into these employment records – not that it was felt desirable to exclude them. It is these employment histories which help to shed light on policy issues about equal opportunities for women and on academic debates about the nature of women's careers, and women's positions within the structures, relations and processes of employment.

PLAN OF THE BOOK

The next chapter documents the distributions of women's employment by occupation, industry and class from the cross-sectional data sources, and outlines several of the major theoretical dilemmas which have been raised by women's employment. Chapter 3 describes the patterns evident in the records of women's occupational changes from the Women and Employment Survey data and draws out the implications for discussions about the nature of women's careers, their occupational choices and their position in the class structure. Chapter 4 documents women's occupational mobility and the implications of these results for labour market theories. Chapter 5 considers the patterns evident in women's mobility between industries along with the implications for theories of the changing structure of employment in Britain. Chapter 6 summarises the main conclusions for theory and policy.

2 The Distributions of Women's Employment

In 1983, 8.8 million women were employed in Britain; 5 million in full-time jobs and 3.8 million in part-time jobs. The full-time figure is a slight decrease on the 1971 figure of 5.5 million although the size of the women's part-time labour force increased by one million, from 2.8 million in 1971. Women's unemployment also grew during the 1970s from 280 700 in 1976 to 854 000 in 1983.[1] The size of the women's labour force as a whole has grown over the post-war period, therefore, and it continued to grow through the 1970s and 1980s recession.

OCCUPATIONS

Women have tended to be located in a narrow range of occupations, notably clerical work, semi-skilled factory work and semi-skilled domestic work; semi-skilled domestic work is likely to be part-time work. In Britain in 1980, 30 per cent of all working women were in clerical jobs, 10 per cent were in semi-skilled factory work and 11 per cent were in semi-skilled domestic work. Of the working women in part-time jobs, however, 20 per cent were in semi-skilled domestic work and only 20 per cent were in clerical jobs.[2] A more detailed table of the distribution of working women by occupation is provided in Table 2.1 from two sources.

Women also constitute a high proportion of certain occupational categories as displayed in Table 2.2. For example, in 1983, women constituted 67 per cent of the professional and related (education, welfare and health), 77 per cent of clerical (non-manual), 59 per cent of selling (non-manual), 76 per cent of catering, cleaning etc. and 45 per cent of painting and repetitive assembling etc. occupations. Women are clearly segregated, therefore, into a small number of occupational categories. More precise measures of this occupational segregation have been developed to capture and measure precisely the extent of this concentration. They are described below.

Women's occupational distribution in other industrialised economies is very similar to that of Britain, with some minor variations.

5

Table 2.1   Occupations of employed women, 1981 Census (10% sample) and WES

	%		*Full-time* %	*Part-time* %	*Total* %
Professional and related supporting management: senior national and local government	2.0	Professional	1	1	1
Professional and related in (education, welfare and health)	12.8	Teaching	8	3	6
Literary, artistic and sports	0.9	Nursing, medical and social	7	6	7
Professional and related (science engineering, technology, etc.)	0.9	Other intermediate non-manual	9	3	6
Managerial	5.3				
Clerical and related	30.2	Clerical	39	20	30
Selling	8.7	Sales	6	12	9
Security and protective service	0.6	Skilled manual	8	6	7

Catering, cleaning, hair dressing and other personal service	20.6	Semi-skilled factory	13	7	10
Farming, fishing and related	0.6	Semi-skilled domestic	4	20	11
Materials processing, making and repairing	5.8	Other semi-skilled	3	5	4
Processing making, repairing (metal and electrical)	1.6	Unskilled	2	17	9
Painting, repetitive assembly product inspection, packing and related	4.2				
Construction, mining and related	1.1				
Transport operating, materials moving and storing					
Miscellaneous	0.5				
Inadequately described	4.2				
Total	100		100	100	100
N (thousands)	987 888		1.877	1.477	3.354

1981 Census

Women and Employment Survey 1980

Table 2.2   Women as a percentage of the occupational labour force in 1983

	%
Non-manual – all	51.4
Managerial (General Management)	8.8
Professional and related supporting management and administration	17.3
Professional and related (education, welfare & health)	66.6
Literary, artistic and sports	30.7
Professional and related (science, engineer, technology)	8.6
Managerial (excluding General)	14.9
Clerical and related	76.7
Selling	58.8
Security and protective service	7.3
Manual – all	29.2
Clerical and related	13.6
Selling	15.4
Security and protective service	22.5
Catering, cleaning, hairdressing and other personal service	76.0
Farming, fishing & related	11.4
Materials processing (excluding metals)	23.9
Making and repairing (excluding metal and electrical)	34.3
Processing, making, repairing and related	4.8
Painting, repetitive assembling, product packaging and related	45.4
Construction, mining etc.	0.7
Transport operating	5.0
Miscellaneous	7.5
Total	40.9

Sources: New Earnings Survey; EOC (1984), figure 3.4, p. 80.

American women, for example, are also heavily concentrated in clerical occupations although Americans are somewhat more likely than British women to be employed in clerical occupations, but also American women have higher proportions than British as women professionals, teachers or in higher grade non-manual occupations. British women were less likely to be employed as skilled manual workers and more likely to be in semi-skilled factory work, sales, semi-skilled domestic and unskilled work. In summary, American women were more likely to be in better-paying occupations than British women, although the differences are not great (Dex and Shaw, 1986). British women also have the highest proportion out of European and North American women, in part-time work (Dex and Shaw, 1986).

OCCUPATIONAL SEGREGATION

Women are clearly concentrated into a small number of occupations and they constitute a very large proportion of certain occupational categories, as noted above. Researchers are agreed that the majority of jobs can be categorised either as stereotypically female, or stereotypically male. Precise measures of the extent to which women are concentrated across the occupational distribution have been developed, partly in order to examine occupational segregation over time to see if it has been changing. When the different measures have been calculated, they suggest that different amounts of occupational segregation exist, at any point in time. The consistent use of any one of these measures to the changing occupational distribution over time provides conclusions about those changes which do not vary according to the measure used however.

The measures of occupational segregation which have been suggested by British and American researchers include the following:

1. The proportion of occupations in which no woman (or man) is employed, as Hakim (1979) suggested.
2. The proportion of occupations in which women form a higher proportion of the workforce than they do in the population. It is possible to make a more sophisticated measure using this method if certain prespecified characteristics which are thought to influence the occupational distributions (e.g. education) are added into the calculation of what the expected distribution would look like.
3. An index of segregation based on the index of similarity or dissimilarity used in social mobility tables has been suggested by Joseph (1983) since, unlike some of the other measures, it is not influenced by the relative (or marginal) numbers in each occupational category.
4. The proportion of occupations in which a certain percentage of the incumbents are women. The percentages used in some US studies have included 70 per cent, 32.8 per cent and 45 per cent. They

show the arbitrary nature of the criterion used. American studies have more recently been using the concepts of 'typical' and 'atypical' occupations for women provided by Jusenius (1976), where a 'typical' occupation is one which has at least 41.3 per cent of its incumbents as women. An 'atypical' occupation is one which has fewer that 33.1 per cent of its incumbents as women; occupations which fall outside both categories tend to be ignored. The percentages are derived by adding or subtracting 5 per cent to or from the proportion of women in the labour force in 1970.

Hakim (1979) has added to this an important distinction between horizontal and vertical occupational segregation. Horizontal segregation occurs if women and men are working in different types of occupations, whereas vertical segregation exists if men are mostly working in higher grade occupations and women in lower grade ones. Blau (1975) added a further distinction between interoccupational segregation – that is, between occupational categories – and intraoccupational segregation, within an occupational category.

Hakim's (1979) calculations of occupational segregation measures illustrated that the extent of segregation depends upon the measure used. Nevertheless, the measures provide useful comparisons over time and for this purpose the broad conclusions are not dependent upon which measure is chosen. Hakim (1979) made comparisons between occupational segregation in Britain and the USA over this century and found that similar conclusions applied to both. They are as follows:

1. Britain and the USA are alike in so far as women are concentrated into occupations which are disproportionately 'female'.
2. Over the period 1900–70 a greater amount of change can be seen in the USA than in Britain. US women had higher participation rates than British women by 1970 and the over-representation of women in disproportionately 'female' jobs declined in the USA between 1900 and 1970 to a greater extent than occurred in Britain. The USA started off having more occupational segregation than Britain but overtook Britain by 1961 in progress towards occupational desegregation.
3. Occupational segregation has not changed very much in Britain over this century.
4. The changing pattern of the occupational distribution was similar in Britain and the USA between 1940 and 1970. Women have been increasingly employed in clerical, sales and service-work

occupations, and women constitute the whole of the private household workers in both countries.

5. The proportion of women in professional work (lower and higher grades) declined in both countries between 1940 and 1970.

6. The changes in occupational segregation which occurred up to 1970 in Britain and the USA are similar, men having made inroads into women's occupations, but the reverse had not occurred to the same extent.

Hakim (1981) updated British work on this issue and Beller (1982, 1982a), England (1982) and Shaw (1983a) have updated the American discussion of this issue, providing measures of occupational segregation in the 1970s. It is interesting to see that the changes which have occurred in the 1970s are still similar in both countries. The studies all found that occupational segregation had declined from 1967 up until 1977. The American studies identified the main source of change as being women's increased probability of working in a 'male' occupation, particularly professional and managerial jobs. Recession in both countries was also thought to have caused women's position to deteriorate later in the 1970s decade. Most of these writers attribute the improvements to legislation about equal opportunities in both countries, although in the USA this source of improvement has been debated.

Despite some improvements, occupational segregation remains widespread. If one adds in intraoccupational segregation from studies like that of Blau (1975), the extent of women's segregation is even greater. The Women and Employment Survey confirmed the widespread nature of women's intraoccupational segregation in Britain (Martin and Roberts, 1984). They found that occupational segregation at the workplace is much higher in Britain than is indicated by studies of the national distribution of occupations, and that 63 per cent of women were in jobs done only by women. The equivalent figure for men is as high as 80 per cent. Martin and Roberts also found that higher-level occupations were less likely to find women working only with women and women were much more likely to work only with women if they worked part-time in any occupation. The extent of occupational segregation appears to increase because of part-time work, although when occupations are controlled for, the increase attributable to part-time work was quite small. The major determinant of the extent of occupational segregation, therefore, is concentration of women in certain occupations rather than in part-time jobs *per se*.

The introduction of occupational segregation and the analysis using this concept have provided us with a much clearer and more accurate description of sexually divided labour markets. We can also see the extent of this division and its relative lack of change over a century of women's employment. The processes by which occupational segregation arises and persists can be seen to be very subtle and very deep-seated. Cockburn's (1985) research has documented some of the micro level divisions; men were found to be willing to sweep the floor with a broom but not with a mop, since the latter was regarded as 'women's work'. Attempts have been made to construct labour market theories of the occupational distributions and the sexual division of labour at a macro level, however; these are reviewed later in this chapter.

INDUSTRIES

Women are disproportionately employed in service industries in Britain. In 1980, 77 per cent of working women were employed in services, and 82 per cent of part-time working women were employed in services (Martin and Roberts, 1984, p. 24). This is the result of a steady growth in the employment of services over the post-war era and a decline in manufacturing employment. The industry which employs a very large proportion of women is the professional and scientific services industry. In 1983, 26.4 per cent of female manual workers, 30.4 per cent of female non-manual workers were employed in this one category.[3] A detailed breakdown of the distribution of working women by industry in 1980 is provided in Table 2.3.

Women are also located in the service sector in other industrialised economies. In the USA, for example, women are more likely to be employed in services and consequently less likely to be employed in manufacturing than British women. However, American women's services jobs are not part-time to the same extent as British women's jobs. Within the service industries, British women are more concentrated in miscellaneous services and American women are more often in insurance and public sector jobs (Dex and Shaw, 1986).

Women also dominate the working populations of certain industry groups. Their concentration in certain industries can be seen from the figures in Table 2.4. In the case of manufacturing industries, women constitute as much as 70 per cent of the labour force in the footwear, clothing and leather industry, 46 per cent of textiles, 36 per cent of

Table 2.3   Industry group of full- and part-time working women in 1980

	Full time	% Part time	Total
Food, drink and tobacco processing	4	3	3
Textiles, clothing and footwear	6	4	5
Engineering and metal manufacturing	10	5	8
Other manufacturing	7	3	5
Total manufacturing	27	15	21
Distribution	14	18	16
Professional and scientific services	25	30	28
Insurance, banking and public administration	16	8	12
Other services	17	26	21
Total services	72	82	77
Agriculture, forestry, fishing, mining, quarrying	1	3	2
Total	100	100	100
N =	1877	1477	3354

Source: from WES data, Martin and Roberts (1984, table 3.4).

food, drink etc. and 37 per cent of other manufacturing. Women have higher concentrations in services however; they constitute 71 per cent of the labour force of the professional and scientific services, 61 per cent of both hotels and catering, and miscellaneous services, and 55 per cent of retail distribution.

This concentration in certain industry groups overlaps with the concentrations of women in occupational categories which were described earlier. The processes by which certain occupations come to be thought of as women's work have an industrial counterpart therefore. It is not coincidental that women's occupations are located primarily in service industries, which are the growth sector of the British economy; women are also heavily concentrated in public sector industries and in a restricted set of manufacturing industries. Theories which have examined Britain's industrial structure initially tended to

Table 2.4   Women as a percentage of the industrial labour force in
1983: Great Britain

	%
Agriculture, forestry and fishing	18.4
Coal and coke	3.6
Extraction of mineral oil and natural gas	17.1
Mineral oil processing	13.3
Other energy and water supply	20.7
Metals	13.3
Other minerals and mineral products	19.3
Chemical industry	27.5
Production of man-made fibres	33.7
Manufacture of metal goods not elsewhere specified	22.5
Mechanical engineering	14.8
Electrical engineering	31.1
Manufacture of motor vehicles and parts thereof	11.6
Manufacture of other transport equipment	10.8
Instrument engineering	31.8
Food, drink and tobacco manufacturing	36.1
Textile industry	45.8
Footwear, clothing and leather	70.3
Timber and wooden furniture industries	18.0
Manufacture of paper products, printing and publishing	30.8
Processing of rubber and plastics	27.6
Other manufacturing industries	37.2
Construction	8.2
Wholesale distribution and commission agents	30.4
Hotels and catering	61.4
Retail distribution and repair of consumer goods and vehicles	54.9
Transport and communication	18.8
Banking, finance, insurance, business services and leasing	48.5
Public administration, national defence and compulsory social security	41.5
Professional and scientific services	70.7
Miscellaneous services	61.1
All industries	40.9

Source: New Earnings Survey 1983, EOC (1984, p. 81).

ignore the gendered divisions. The importance of these divisions for understanding the industrial changes is now being recognised. We shall return to this theme in Chapter 5.

SEGMENTED LABOUR MARKETS

One attempt to theorise about the distributions of gender groups by occupation and industry has come from the segmented labour market theories. Theories of segmented labour markets began to appear in the USA in the 1960s, but their roots are often traced back to the 1950s' institutionalist economists and perhaps more significantly to classical economists like Cairnes and J. S. Mill. Segmented labour markets were offered as a distinct alternative to neoclassical labour-market models in 1960s, and they were claimed to be superior in the understanding they offered of persistent wage differentials, occupational segregation, poverty, and race and sex discrimination. Segmented labour market theories link together pay differentials with these other phenomena and offer an explanation of the whole.[4]

There are now a wide variety of segmented labour-market models as Loveridge and Mok's (1979) review illustrates. They vary mainly in the number of segments they describe and in the criteria which characterise and identify the different segments. The initial and most simple dual labour market model described two labour markets, but this was soon replaced by further division, although the name 'dual labour market' is often still used of the whole genre of these models, irrespective of the exact number of segments. We can examine here the most popularly cited model, the Piore model, in order to see the essential elements of segmented labour-market theories.

Piore's (1975) model of a segmented labour market has two main sectors, but one is subdivided further giving three segments in all. The first major division between the primary and secondary sector is described by Piore (1975, p. 126) as follows:

> The basic hypothesis of the dual labor market was that the labor market is divided into two essentially distinct sectors, termed primary and secondary sectors. The former offers jobs with relatively high wages, good working conditions, chances of advancement, equity and due process in the administration of work rules and above all, employment stability. Jobs in the secondary sector, by contrast, tend to be low paying, with poor working conditions, little chance of advancement, a highly personalised relationship between

workers and supervisors which leads to wide latitude for favouritism and is conducive to hard and capricious work discipline and with considerable instability in jobs and a high turnover among the labor force.

Workers compete within each market for jobs, wages and employment conditions in general. Mobility barriers prohibit the movement of workers from the secondary sector to the primary market. The theory concerns itself, therefore, with the occupational as well as pay divisions in labour markets.

Piore introduced a further division within the primary sector to counter the view that the initial dual formulation of the theory focused too narrowly on the problems of disadvantaged workers at the expense of equally important distinctions between primary jobs. Thus, he suggested an upper or 'primary independent' sector, composed of professional and managerial jobs. These were distinct from the lower tier 'subordinate primary jobs' by their higher pay, higher mobility and turnover patterns which, in some ways, resembled those of the secondary sector. Formal education was a requirement of jobs in the upper primary sector and thus constituted an absolute barrier to entry into these prestigious jobs. The lower primary tier might contain low-level non-manual jobs or craft-based manual jobs, but they would have much less variety in the context of their work and little opportunity for individual creativity and initiative. The characteristics of the work in the three sectors, Piore thought, were closely related to sociological distinctions between the lower-, working- and middle-class sub-cultures, so one of the essential and interesting elements of this theory is that job characteristics and workers' characteristics match each other – at least they do after workers have started their jobs. The majority of women are part of the secondary sector workforce and this is offered as, in large part, the explanation of their lower pay.

This basic description of labour-market segments is accepted by all writers in this school; writers diverge more in their views about the causes of segmentation in labour markets, although they all see it as part of a historical process. An early work by Doeringer and Piore (1971) described the development of an 'internal labour market', which was suggested to be a feature of the primary market, and its development arose through the negotiation process between labour and management, alongside changes in industrial structure and technology. An internal labour market is one where the competition between prospective candidates for a job is restricted to those already employed in the firm. An internal labour market thus charts out a career structure. It has obviously been in the interests of management and unions to promote the construction of internal labour markets; for unions, they provide better conditions of work, promotion prospects and greater security of employment; for management, they offer a stable workforce which, if training or recruitment costs are high, minimises these costs and reduces the cost of labour turnover. While the specific reasons for this development are not formalised into a theory by the authors, it has tended to be assumed that internal labour markets and the primary sector of which they are a part have developed alongside oligopolistic markets, unionised and highly capitalised production processes. Secondary jobs, therefore, are thought to be located in unconcentrated industries and competitive firms. The sectoral division is sometimes described as one between the core, large-scale monopolised firms, and the periphery, small-scale competitive marginalised industries.

The segmented labour-market theories were imported into Britain largely through two papers: one by Doeringer and Bosanquet (1973) and one by Barron and Norris (1976); the latter looked specifically at the role of women. Barron and Norris adopted the dualistic framework and suggested that the main motivation for primary labour markets to develop was the need for firms to retain their scarce skilled workforce, to reduce its turnover and to circumvent disruptive demands for better pay and working conditions. They then suggested that women workers fitted the description of the secondary workforce since they had lower pay, that they were concentrated in unskilled and insecure jobs, that they were more likely to be made redundant than men and less likely to be upwardly mobile. Moreover, women were said to have the necessary attributes which made them a suitable secondary workforce; namely, they are meant to be easily dispensible, they do not value economic rewards highly, they are easily identifiable as a group, they are not very ambitious to acquire training or work experience and they are relatively ununionised and unlikely to develop solidaristic links with their fellow workers. Rubery (1978) elaborated this framework in the context of the British division of labour, and Ryan (1981) clarified how empirical work could help to resolve some of the problems embedded in testing these theories.

There have been some empirical studies of segmented labour markets in Britain. Blackburn and Mann's (1979) study of Peterborough is probably the most famous, but it largely excludes women and it examined segmentation between men's work only. There have been a growing number of smaller-scale empirical analyses of sexual segregation and these are helping to uncover some of the processes whereby segmentation is constructed and maintained (Coyle, 1982; Armstrong, 1982; Craig *et al*. 1982; Craig and Wilkinson, 1985; Rubery and Wilkinson, 1979; Lawson, 1981; Freeman, 1982; Robinson and Wallace, 1984). These studies have highlighted the importance of the capital intensity of production, trade union bargaining power, the composition of trade unions, product demand and variability and the role of paternalistic relations for understanding women's position in both the occupational and industrial structure in Britain. Some more quantitative British studies and tests of the segmented labour market concept are now beginning to emerge (Brown, 1983; Dale *et al*., 1984); these parallel the American developments in this field.[5]

To some extent, the more recent studies have tackled some of the criticisms which were levelled against segmented labour market theories, in particular by feminist critics. For example, Beechey (1978) argued that segmentation theories were not specific enough to women's position in the industrial and occupational structures, tended to treat all women as homogeneous, and they were static and ahistorical. Rubery (1978) was critical of the omission of worker's organisation. However, we are still some way from describing a set of labour market segments which do reflect women's position sufficiently well to be able to predict the outcome of changes. At the core segmented labour market theories are concerned, on the employee side, with lifetime mobility between jobs, or the lack of such; yet such data have been unavailable in Britain until recently. There is much scope for further analyses, therefore, which focus on integrating women's lifetime job mobility into theories of labour market processes. The WES data on women's work histories presented in subsequent chapters has a contribution to make to this task.

CLASS ANALYSIS

The role of women has become a major issue in sociological theorising about class relations in industrial societies. Some theories of class have relied upon the occupational classification of workers, that is male workers, in order to identify their class categorisation. Men's occupations were then used as a basis for classifying their whole family or household. Feminist critics pointed out that this procedure involved an assumption either that women did not work, or, if they did, that their occupations were not important in determining the class of the family (Acker, 1980). The increasing importance of the women's labour force has forced this issue onto the agenda although there is no agreement about how the issues can be resolved.[6] Some confusion has been generated by critics' failing to recognise the very different traditions of class analysis in America and Europe. This review concentrates on the European tradition of class analysis, which builds largely on the Marxian and Marxist analyses of class.[7]

Much of class analysis can be described as being an attempt to identify the boundaries of social groups or categories which are called 'classes' (MacKenzie, 1982). Within this tradition there have been a number of attempts to incorporate women, although all have been criticised as inadequate by feminists.

Poulantzas (1973) is one of the writers who has been attempting to provide a sophisticated theory of social change which relates to twentieth-century developments; in particular, which relates to changes in labour-market relationships, Poulantzas's theory suggests that there are three levels in a class society: economic, political and ideological. While classes are primarily determined in the economic sphere, they contain strong elements of political and ideological elements. In Poulantzas, each class has a 'place' in the structure of relations and a 'position' in a conjuncture; that is, a position in the specific historical situation. The economic basis of classes is defined by their relation to production; in particular, whether a class is engaged in productive or unproductive labour. Poulantzas introduces a further new concept, 'a class fraction'; that is, part of a class which can ally itself with sections of other classes. Poulantzas's conceptual discussion reduces to a description of three social classes in society: the bourgeoisie, the working class and a 'new middle strata' containing the old and new petty bourgeoisie.

As far as women are concerned, Poulantzas recognised that women constitute much of the new white-collar labour which forms part of the new middle strata. This middle-class contains three major fractions: low-level sales and service workers, bureaucratised workers in banking, administration, the civil service and education, and low-level technicians and engineers. Much of the discussion has centred on whether this new class are likely to ally with the proletariat or the bourgeoisie. Women's occupancy of some of these new class positions has been used in arguments both to reject and accept the embourgeoisement (or proletarianisation) theories.

West (1978) criticised Poulantzas. She suggests that Poulantzas fails to explain why the agents who are filling the class positions and who are becoming increasingly deskilled are mainly women. There are also inconsistencies in Poulantzas's treatment of the sexual division of labour since, at one and the same time, women are regarded as secondary and an important component of the new petty bourgeois class. Women's domestic role is unconsidered by Poulantzas. Poulantzas, whilst considering the contemporary labour-market divisions, fails to consider the question of how sexual divisions affect the class structure.

Wright (1978) criticised Poulantzas but uses his notion of a class fraction. Wright's unique contribution is the suggestion that many positions in the social division of labour will be ambiguous. These ambiguous positions should be recognised as such and given the title of 'objectively contradictory locations within class relations'. Apparently, 50 per cent of the population of advanced capitalist societies appear to be in this contradictory location. Wright also attempted to overcome Poulantzas's more static analysis by providing a historical analysis of the development of capitalism, explaining why these contradictory locations within the class structure have arisen. Three types of structural changes were identified as contributing to their emergence; the progressive loss of control over the labour process by direct producers, the progressive differentiation of the functions of capital and the development of complex hierarchies of control within business. In the end, however, Wright's approach is static and mechanical (MacKenzie, 1982), and he has seven categories, replacing the three in Poulantzas, to which individuals are allocated largely according to their occupations.

Wright attempted to incorporate women into his class structure, but women who are not employed at the (cross-section) time he is describing in the US class structure are ignored. Wright argues that these non-employed women have a class position which is mediated through their husbands. Women who are employed are given an individual class position since Wright believes that the individual is the appropriate unit for describing the class structure. He is then able to divide his sample by sex and compare the class distributions of each sex through his seven categories.

Wright has offered a partial solution to the problem of recognising women in the class structure. His solution incorporates women who happen to be employed when he decides to describe the class structure. Since most women are likely to be employed at some time in their lives, Wright's approach does not capture the dynamics of women's employment. Wright's class analysis is not one which integrates the sexual division of labour nor women's domestic labour, largely because of its static and boundary-drawing nature. Carchedi (1975, 1977) has attempted to develop Wright's analysis, but he has nothing new to offer as far as women are concerned. Other American Marxist analyses have been generated through a consideration of labour markets; for example Bowles and Gintis (1975, 1976) and Edwards, Reich and Gordon (1975).

Radical economists like Edwards, Reich and Gordon (1975) have offered a much more specific theory of the development of segmented markets which shares the description of the segments noted above but clearly locates segmentation in the political and economic forces of American capitalism. They suggest that labour-market segmentation arises in the historical transition from competitive capitalism, with its tendencies towards homogeneous labour and that this has led to tensions and strikes; monopoly capitalism is the outcome. Segmentation, therefore, is seen as part of a conscious effort by employers to overcome labour tendencies and should be part, therefore, of a class analysis. Once segmentation is established, it is maintained by the interdependence which grows up between the sectors through large-scale core monopoly firms contracting out their unstable production to peripheral secondary-sector industries. The theorists suggest that segmentation is functional to the perpetuation of capitalist institutions and it prevents workers from uniting to overthrow these institutions. In so far as these radical theories build upon segmented labour market theories they have some of the same limitations, as far as women's work is concerned, as do other theories under this heading described above.

However, some important questions remain unanswered by these Marxist analyses. What, in the logic of capitalist development, causes the changes in the sexual division of labour, like women's growing monopoly of new service jobs? What, in this same logic, makes employers stop short of employing more women if they are so much cheaper? The failure to consider these important questions about social change has led critics to suggest that Marxists have lost sight of Marx's method of analysis, which was essentially historical. In so far as they continue to seek to provide static descriptions of class boundaries, they will not be able to offer an integral theory of class analysis and sexual inequalities (MacKenzie, 1982). Marxist-feminist writers have been attempting to steer the tradition towards other goals which would address these questions.

Giddens has become a major British contributor to the study of class analysis. The main problem which Giddens addressed was: 'How can one go from a recognition of the diversity of market capacities of individuals to classes as structured forms?' It is the problem of relating Marx's abstract model to specific societal analyses but phrased in terms more like a Weberian view of classes. Classes, in Weber, were defined in terms of their market position. Giddens avoids an overly static conception of the class structure by wanting to talk about the degree to which societies have class structuration. By 'class structuration' he means 'the modes in which "economic" relationships become translated into "non-economic" social structures' (1973, p. 105). Nevertheless he is contributing to the discussion of class boundaries. The structuration of class relationships, as a variable, depends upon two types of influence: mediate and proximate structuration. Mediate structuration includes factors like the amount of social mobility or the degree of closure of mobility chances, or the ownership of property or qualifications. Proximate structuration influences are the localised factors influencing class formation like the division of labour within productive enterprises, authority relations and consumption differences between groups. Giddens shares with Goldthorpe and Parkin the interest in defining class boundaries, at least partly, in terms of individuals' mobility chances. Although Giddens does not say so, one suspects he means, like Goldthorpe and Parkin, *men's* mobility chances.

Women enter Giddens's analysis in a number of ways. In what has become a well-quoted passage, he suggests: 'Given that women still have to await their liberation from the family, it remains the case in the capitalist societies that female workers are largely peripheral to the class system; or expressed differently, women are in a sense the "underclass" of the white-collar sector' (1973, p. 288).

Goldthorpe (1983), in defence of Giddens, has commented on this point, and suggested that Giddens's statement derives directly from a premise which feminists would not wish to deny, even though they end up being critical of Giddens. There may well have been some criticism of Giddens by feminists which was on misplaced grounds, but there is a point which remains undefended in Giddens's writing. It concerns the inconsistency of maintaining, as he does here, that women are peripheral, and suggesting, in other discussions in the same work, that women are part of a central and new concept introduced to help reconceptualise Marxian analysis – the buffer zone between the old bourgeoisie and proletariat classes. Women are brought into Giddens's discussion to argue against the idea that a progressive embourgeoisement of the working class has been taking place, but they are not integrated more positively into the analysis, and inconsistencies about women's positions thus arise.

Giddens's point that women's dependence on men in families makes them peripheral is a direct example of Allen's (1982) criticism that certain assumptions preclude further examination. We do not know the extent to which women are dependent upon their husbands, especially since the majority of women now go out to work and most of them work for 60 per cent or more of their potential working lives (Martin and Roberts, 1984, pp. 202–3). Giddens may be accurately portraying women's employment as often semi-skilled with little training, few prospects, part-time and low-paid. But calling this marginal or secondary work misses the point, as West (1978) notes; irregular labour can be vital rather than marginal to the whole economic system. In a recent book edited by Giddens and MacKenzie (1982) an article by MacKenzie looks hopefully to the labour-market analysis of American radical economists for a future integration of a dynamic theory which incorporates human action along with structural analysis and women's roles. Giddens appears to recognise the lack of development in this field, therefore; it presumably will continue until the nettle is grasped.

Goldthorpe has contributed to class analysis in Britain through the empirical examination of social mobility (1980). He illustrated that social mobility has been considered as a negative force, precluding the formation of classes and as potentially destabilising and therefore undesirable. Goldthorpe sees social mobility within a conflict model of society as desirable but possibly destabilising. He treats the relationship of social mobility to class formation as an empirical issue. Goldthorpe *et al.* have described the class structure of Britain in the 1970s and 1980s on the basis of detailed empirical analyses of the intergenerational and intragenerational social mobility of British men. They have thus been involved in a description of class boundaries but in the process have modified some of the alternative theoretical concepts.

Goldthorpe shares a concept of class with other Weberian writers like Parkin, and they both see the class system as 'a set of institutional arrangements which guarantee a fairly high degree of social continuity in the reward position of family units through generations' (Parkin, 1971, p. 14). Both writers also see the family as the appropriate social unit of the class system, and the occupational system as the backbone of the class structure. Since the family is adopted as the unit of class analysis, women's class position is indicated by their husband's position. The effective exclusion of women from class analysis which this entails has been justified on grounds of expediency (Goldthorpe 1980, Appendix); more recently it has been made a virtue by Goldthorpe (1983), who has engaged in a debate with feminist critics of traditional class analysis.

The necessity and relevance of information about the occupational experiences of women over their lifetime becomes obvious when we begin to evaluate the tradition of class analysis as a whole, and some of the very contemporary debates. One solution to the problem of how to incorporate women into class analysis, offered by Wright (1978), was to adopt the individual as the appropriate class unit. Women can then be incorporated into class analysis according to their occupation when they are employed, but they are ignored if they are not employed. The use of the individual as a unit of class analysis is at best a partial solution to the objective of integrating sexual inequalities into class analysis. A development which has involved a greater change in class analysis has come from suggesting that the family be kept as the unit of class analysis but that the categories used to describe the class structure change to incorporate both men's and women's occupations. The list of categories for these analyses allow men and women to be in the same occupational category or to be in different categories; in the latter case they are called 'cross-class families'. Britten and Heath (1983) have provided the most extensive description of a class structure using both men's and women's occupations and allowing cross-class categories. They allow men and women to be unemployed in their classification. Their empirical analysis also demonstrates that there are correlations between their categories and the voting behaviour of their samples. They suggest that these correlations are evidence that their categories are identifying genuine social groups out of their samples.

Goldthorpe (1983) has presented an empirical analysis to offer a defence of the traditional class analysis. He has claimed that the practice of taking the family as a unit of class analysis, using the head of household's (usually male) occupation to indicate the class position and assuming that a wife's class status is the same as that of her husband, best fits the empirical facts of family structure in Britain. He draws these conclusions from an analysis of the wives of the men in the Oxford Mobility Study; in particular, he examined the wives' employment histories alongside the social mobility experiences of their husbands. Goldthorpe suspects that he would be prepared to alter his view if the facts were different.[8] Goldthorpe makes clear in his discussions that the debate does not rest upon the issue of whether women are dependent upon men in marriage; on this both sides agree.

On the basis of his empirical work, supplemented by other women's work-history data, he concluded that women's labour-market attachment is still too intermittent to entitle them to a class classification in their own right; women's occupational mobility is such that they cannot be regarded as holding a class position in terms of the continuity required for class formation and classification. Goldthorpe also suggests that cross-class families are rather rare.

There have been several replies to Goldthorpe's defence. Stanworth (1984) challenges Goldthorpe's empirical work and the conclusion he draws from it. Stanworth points out that Goldthorpe does not provide any evidence that a wife's employment is conditioned by her husband's employment. Heath and Britten (1984) and Goldthorpe (1984) have continued to debate these points and it is clear that they agree on many points. There are still unresolved differences between them which appear to be ones of defining the nature of class analysis. For Goldthorpe, class analysis is about identifying stable collectivities which, he suggests, will not necessarily coincide with either socio-cultural differentiation or with socio-political mobilisation and conflict. In this case the dispute must be about the criteria for identifying both a collectivity, and stability. None of the parties consider the parallel problems for men's class identification of men's mass unemployment nowadays.

The issues are far from being resolved to everyone's satisfaction. Some researchers are suggesting that class analysis should be reconceptualised in such a way as to eliminate these debates (Walby, 1984; Leonard and Delphy, 1984). Walby's (1984) suggestion that class analysis should focus on relations within households, however, is not necessarily an alternative to recognising class relations between employers and employees. We can accept from these authors, that all class relations emerge within a framework where both patriarchal and capitalist relations are manifest and intersect. It is important that patriarchal relations are not ignored or assumed secondary to class relations.

Some resolution to these traditional issues could emerge if several empirical questions could be answered. The data required to tackle these questions were unavailable until recently, and the debates have often used cross-sectional data on women's employment. Women's employment over the lifecycle is undoubtedly intermittent in that breaks from work occur, not least for childbirth. However, most women do appear to be permanently attached to the labour force these days since they intend to return to work after childbirth (Martin and Roberts, 1984). Part of the problem of providing a class category for women stumbled over what to do with those currently not employed. If women's occupational experiences over their lifetimes were sufficiently clearly defined it would be possible to provide an occupational, and subsequently a class classification of their experiences based on past occupations. Whether this is possible is an empirical question which can only be resolved by the availability of suitable longitudinal data on women's work histories; whether women's part-time work affects the ability to provide such a classification is also an empirical issue. The necessary data for addressing these questions became available in WES. This type of lifetime record also holds out the possibility of beginning to investigate another empirical question; of how far a wife's employment is dependent upon her husband's employment. These issues will be examined in the chapters which follow.

CONCLUSIONS

Explanations of occupational segregation and theories about the place of women in labour markets and in the class structure all share the characteristics of being incomplete. Researchers are all noting the importance to the theories of resolving the issue of how and where women fit in; some progress is being made. Walby (1985), for example, listed the main explanations of occupation segregation as the impact of the family on women's work, a combination of family and ideological influences on women and men, segmented labour market theories and the interrelationship of capitalist and patriarchal structures. After examining the first three explanations, finding that they do not fit the facts sufficiently well, Walby argued for a development of the last explanation which builds largely on the work of American feminist Hartmann, although she suggests that the best elements of other approaches should also be drawn in.[9]

Theories of occupational segregation, of labour market operations and of class analysis have tended, as far as women are concerned, to be built largely upon the cross-sectional picture of women's employment. (Some research has drawn in the historical changes in the cross-sectional distributions). Theoretical work in these areas has suffered from the lack of information about women's employment experiences over time. One could argue that the equivalent information about men's experiences would also be valuable, irrespective of whether they have stable or intermittent employment patterns. Stewart, Prandy and Blackburn (1980) have noted that problems arise for attempts at theorising because the occupational classification is very uneven as it stands; some occupations reflect lifetime profiles (tracks on a railway line) whilst others are short stopping places (i.e. stations).

The work history experiences of women in the WES data enable us to begin to fill in more of this micro picture of women's occupational experiences; it is also a more dynamic picture, highlighting the mechanisms of occupational segregation as they operate through individuals' and households' experiences and choices. The analysis of the WES data which is presented in later chapters provides, therefore, a better foundation for theorising about labour market relations. It is necessarily incomplete as a contribution to uncovering more about gender relations and how patriarchal and capitalist relations intersect, since the data are wholly women's data; but it is a start.

3 Occupational Profiles

We can now begin to focus on the patterns of women's occupations over time. How do women move between jobs over their lifetimes; if they do? As indicated earlier, most of the existing studies have examined women's location in the occupational structure through cross-sectional information; that is using data on their current occupations. A cross-sectional picture of an occupational distribution will give an accurate picture of women's positions if those positions never change. If women's occupations change over their lifetime, however, the cross-sectional picture will not accurately reflect their lifetime occupational status. The occupational histories of women contained in the Women and Employment Survey (WES) provides the first extensive large scale British data through which to begin to tackle unanswered questions about the nature of women's careers and occupational changes over their lifetime.[1]

Occupational sociology has a tradition of considering careers. As with many sociological traditions, there has been a tendency to focus on men's experiences and the concept of 'a career' has developed in this context and for such usage. More recently the concept of a career has been the subject of critical review and whilst the name has been retained, its range of meanings has been vastly extended. Women's careers have also begun to be considered, although the necessary empirical base required before a meaningful set of career types could be constructed was unavailable until now. We can turn to a brief review of the tradition of 'career' studies as a context for the description of women's occupational experiences which follows.

THE CONCEPT OF CAREER

The concept of 'career' has been central to the study of occupational sociology, although its meaning has undergone modifications and refinements over time. A 'career' seems to suggest some progress through a series of occupations or maybe staying in one occupation over time. At this level the notion is equivalent to a work history and, as such, it would be a descriptive concept. 'Career' has not always been used in this way, however, and the dominant meaning attached to the concept has been prescriptive. Following Hughes (1937), Becker (1970, p. 165) defined a career as 'the patterned series of adjustments made by an individual to the network of institutions, formal organizations and informal relationships in which the work of the occupation is performed'.

Slocum's (1966, p. 5) definition is typical of the prescriptive and hierarchical overtones which became attached to the concept: 'An *occupational career* may be defined for this discussion as an ordered sequence of development extending over a period of years and involving progressively more responsible roles within an occupation'. Slocum's concept is a more abstract and non-empirical concept than earlier notions, as he himself recognised. Empirical work when it took place consisted of case studies of single occupations or investigations of particular aspects of an individual's behaviour or work history, and as such the longitudinal or developmental nature of a career got lost, as did the potential patterns or shared experiences of individuals.

Alongside large numbers of case studies, a theoretical development took place which began to construct typologies of the mass of individual case studies. The typologies set out to reduce the large number of ethnographic accounts to a smaller number of categories which usually had at their basis a division according to how the study resolved a key issue in the organisation of work or careers. For example, Caplow (1954) constructed a typology around the themes of the manner of recruitment, returns to seniority, evaluation of merit and control over occupational behaviour, amongst other issues raised in his investigations. Caplow thus arrived at four categories of occupations. Slocum (1966) also suggested a set of categories which focused on the different institutional environments (e.g. the bureaucratic career), and many others exist, some only being modest variants of the US Census Bureau's major occupational groupings.

Hearn (1977) provided another career typology but as a criticism of earlier forms. Hearn was critical not only of the assumption of any necessary hierarchy in the concept of 'career' but also of whether an ordered sequence was necessarily involved and the conscious, rational pursuit of goals which an ordered sequence implies. Hearn suggested that a typology of careers could be constructed along the two main dimensions of whether jobs are intrinsically meaningful or not and whether work has meaning or no meaning in the wider context. A set of four career types are then possible; the pure career is the career definition of Caplow, where there is a structuring of time in the past and in the future. Hearn's other career types recognise the decline of work as a 'central life interest' and they include 'the careerless' who accept the rules of the game but who do not seriously compete; the 'uncareer', where *both* work and career are neither coherent nor meaningful as seen in the individual's wider environment; and the 'non-career', where work and a career are no longer meaningful in either an immediate or in wider terms. Hearn (1981) extended the range of types to include the 'guerrilla career' and the 'cop-out career', although these are not set within the same dimensions as the first four types. Hearn has successfully extended the notion of a career, detaching its meaning from having a necessary link with upward hierarchical progressions, but he also took a further step away from empirically based typologies. Whereas Caplow and Slocum were constructing typologies to make sense of empirical studies, Hearn, as is the danger with all typologising, is offering typologies of the logical possibilities, although he does try and offer examples to fit each. There are, however, grave dangers in such an approach if it locks our thinking into grooves which have little relation to experiences.

Spilerman (1977) reviews many of these developments in an unfavourable light for a number of reasons. He is critical of the trend away from empirically based career descriptions, and he suggests that where empirical work has taken place, through the ethnographic accounts, there is a bias in the types of career discussed. Most of the accounts are concerned with careers within institutional structures, and few if any consider career lines which traverse institutional boundaries or change maybe in mid-life. As such, the careers described are little help to understanding the determinants of industry structures and labour-market distributions of workers. Spilerman (1977) thinks as does Grandjean (1981) that the very notion of career is and should be about an individual's relationship to the structure of employment; Spilerman (p. 553) sees 'the career notion', therefore, 'as a strategic link between structural features of the labour market and the socio-economic attainments of individuals'.

A recent study of male white-collar employees by Stewart, Prandy and Blackburn (1980) has contributed to the concept of 'career' whilst being primarily about the place of men's clerical work in the class structure. They pointed out how uneven the occupational classification is, particularly as a basis for measuring a man's class affiliation since some occupational categories encapsulate careers over a man's life time; they use the analogy of the railway lines here. Other occupations are merely stops along the way; using the same analogy, these are stations. Stewart *et al.* are critical of Slocum's definition of an occupation because he incorporates the notion of a (railway) line into it and thereby confuses lines and stations. It has not been clear whether it was necessary to make this point about women's occupations, since there were no data on women's occupational mobility over their lifetime with which to examine the issue. Stewart, Prandy and Blackburn (1980) were firmly in the mainstream discussions of occupations and class analysis in paying attention solely to men's employment and only lip-service to the importance of women's work.

Women were neglected by this line of development within the sociology of work. The earlier views of 'career' as a descriptive concept could have incorporated women, and indeed, Hughes (1937, p. 411) pointed out that 'A woman may have a career in holding together a family or in raising it to a new position'. Whilst this view is one which sees women playing only a limited role, it has the virtue of at least putting women's domestic work on a par with men's paid occupations. However, the empirical work of this Chicago tradition did not build upon this foundation. Their commitment to a sociological analysis which recognised the links between jobs, even though some would not be thought of as bona fide occupations or professions by the general public (e.g. call girls), was a foundation upon which a consideration of housework could have built. Unfortunately, their work extended to women only in so far as they were prostitutes, who were not exactly a representative sample of all women. More often women's acceptance of a domestic role had promoted a negative view of their occupational experiences. The quotation from Tyler by Slocum (1966, p. 214) aptly illustrates this point:

A girl may see it as more important that she be acceptable to the kinds of people who matter to her, so that the kind of man she wants to marry will be likely to propose to her than that she find the occupation that best fits her talents and aptitudes.

With the move away from using 'career' in a descriptive sense, even minority women's groups were no longer represented in sociological studies of work. It is not too difficult to see why women were neglected by this line of development within the sociology of work, especially if the discipline initially intended to investigate men's work. If women were more likely to be in the cross-institutional career trajectories, or if they made less obvious progressions up an occupational hierarchy, they would also be more likely to be excluded. As the move away from empirical descriptions of career paths progressed, it would have cemented further the tendency to ignore women, since if women were assumed not to work or have careers, little other than empirical examination would be likely to challenge such a view. Some of Hearn's

(1981) types of career are meant to apply to women, but since they are not derived from empirical work, we can only speculate on their validity.

Spilerman's (1977) reconceptualisation of the notion of 'career' is one which is more open to considering women, but it has come late in the story, when alternative lines of development have now been plotted by feminists and others. It is interesting to note that Spilerman's review of the use of the term 'career' in sociology does not mention the problem of its exclusion of women, and neither does his offered solution specifically include them. There is a sense, therefore, in which part of the tradition of career analysis is still male-centred, but alongside this are a growing number of empirical studies of women (Rosenfeld, 1979, 1980).

There are studies now of women in factory work in a variety of industries (Pollert, 1981; Cavendish, 1982; Purcell, 1979; Wajcman, 1983; Coyle, 1982), of women in the professions (Theodore, 1971), in banking (Llewelyn, 1981), in journalism (Smith, 1976) and of women in clerical and secretarial work (Silverstone, 1974, 1975; McNally, 1979). Studies of women in service occupations and part-time work are currently sparse, although Beechey and Perkins's (1983) unpublished work on part-time work in Coventry will help to fill this gap, and Terkel (1974) includes ethnographic descriptions of hairdressers, waitresses and some other service occupations. The Women and Employment Survey (WES) provides the large scale overview for these smaller scale studies, and it has the advantage of not being tied to particular institutions.

It is worth noting that the WES data found that 17 per cent of all working women said that one of their reasons for working was 'to follow my career'; 24 per cent of full-time workers and 7 per cent of part-time workers gave this response. Only 5 per cent of working women gave this response as their main reason for working (Martin and Roberts, 1984). It might be argued, on the basis of these results, that women themselves are uninterested in a career, just as the stereotype view has held. It is far more likely, however, that these responses reflect women's realistic views of their own limited job opportunities, the constraints of child-care responsibilities, and their own disrupted working lives, especially for those in part-time work. The view of 'a career' which is being used by these women is likely to be one which restricts 'careers' to a few professional occupations, and it is, of course, a fact that few women are employed in professional occupations. A sociological understanding of the term career, as we have seen, seeks to widen the notion and examine the empirical patterns of women's working lives as a better basis for constructing career types.

OCCUPATIONAL CHOICE

One topic which has received separate attention as part of the focus on careers is that of occupational choice. It is obviously of central interest to an individual's career and will specifically involve the consideration of whether individuals have career strategies in any meaningful sense. The development of the study of occupational choice parallels the story told about the concept of 'career' as far as women are concerned. Investigations were made in the 1950s and 1960s of the choice of an initial occupation, usually on leaving school, but later also on graduating from college at the beginning of an individual's labour-market experience. Much of the interest has focused on providing better vocational and careers guidance to school-leavers.

The early studies of occupational choice employed the same assumptions as the study of careers; namely, that an occupation is what one is paid for, and that young women are not that interested in their jobs since they are just filling in time before getting married. The studies of occupational choice reviewed by Caplow (1954) and Slocum (1966) are wholly concerned with young men. A review by Clarke (1980), however, points out that many of the studies of occupational choice from 1968 to 1980 included young women in their samples, but few considered the gender effects on occupational choice.

The early studies broadly saw occupational choice as an event, but as early as 1951 in the work of Ginzberg (1951) and Super (1953), a move began to view occupational choice as a developmental process. Ginzberg's work outlined three phases in the development of young men's occupational choices: the fantasy phase and the tentative phase, followed by the realistic phase, and these became the framework for much of the work which followed. In the late 1960s and 1970s, developments in the UK and USA began to diverge significantly. The work of Blau and Duncan (1967) in the USA confirmed, if not initiated, a strongly quantitative set of investigations into the factors affecting the first occupations of young male workers and their subsequent occupational attainment. In Britain, studies were less quantitative and theoretical debates took the centre of the stage: the British debates considered whether the process was one of occupational choice or occupational allocation (Roberts, 1968, 1973). When women were eventually recognised as an important group, they were incorporated into the analysis on both sides of the Atlantic in a way that was in keeping with the tradition already established in each case. The British studies of occupational choice are reviewed in Clarke (1980, 1980a). Where they are empirical in nature, they use less sophisticated statistical techniques than the US studies, although they reach most of the same conclusions – that home background, ethnic origin and education have strong influences on the level of occupational choices and aspirations of young men, and weaker influences are found from certain family factors and from the geographical environment. Personal characteristics like intelligence or ability, personality, interests, values, occupational knowledge and, in the few cases where it was included, sex, were all found to be important variables.

A theoretical debate took the centre stage of British sociological interest in occupational choice in the 1970s. A debate arose about whether this process of occupational choice actually involved a rational and conscious choice from a range of known alternatives. Roberts (1968, 1973) was one of the prime critics of the choice idea, suggesting instead that the process was one of allocating individuals to jobs. The idea of an allocation process was meant to suggest that an individual is almost powerless in the situation and that factors beyond his control are determining his fate. The empirical evidence that working-class children get working-class jobs and middle-class ones get middle-class jobs etc. was used to support the idea of the allocation process. About the same time a similar set of points began to be made in the USA by the radical economists Bowles and Gintis (1976) about US education, but their attack was directed largely towards orthodox economic analysis and formed a part of the segmented labour-market literature, so it had less impact on US sociological interest in occupational choice.

The debate in Britain was not fully resolved, although it did die out and things moved on. A study of working-class boys by Willis (1977) illustrated that the so-called allocation process was complex and that it included active resistance to school culture on the part of working-class boys. Paradoxically, this resistance permitted the boys to adjust easily into the work culture of mundane and low-skilled working-class jobs. Little discussion can be found in this debate about girls or young women's occupational choices; they are either ignored, or workers and young people are treated as unisex, as we saw previously.

Some empirical studies of young women were taking place in the 1970s, and these are gradually starting to fill in the gaps about how British young women choose occupations and make the transition to work (e.g. McRobbie, 1978; McRobbie and Garber, 1975; Sherratt, 1983). Oakley's (1974, 1979) work is also beginning to uncover the sense and ways in which young women choose motherhood or housework as an occupation. This latter development has taken place since the waged versus unwaged divide has been broken down and women's occupations have been added to the list of occupations. Empirical studies are beginning to give us an understanding of women's occupational choice, and as with other fields, the picture turns out to be far from the stereotyped assumptions about young women which dominated and precluded serious study for so long. Sherratt (1983) found from a small sample of young women taking up FE that there was little evidence of any kind that they had a domestic orientation, but instead an orientation in which getting a paid job was central. Their concept of 'glamour' goes a long way towards explaining their occupational choices, and even through their failure to achieve their aspirations, they remained orientated to working and ended up in so-called women's jobs with low pay.

A feminist interest in women's occupational choice has also injected something into the debate on allocation versus choice. It is that both of these aspects of occupations must be considered and are important particularly for women. This view suggests that it is erroneous to see any process wholly deterministically since it is important to allow the actors to play an active rather than a passive role – in this case young women are the actors.

We can see, in these traditions of sociological research, a tendency to neglect women although this is starting to be rectified. The description of women's occupational experiences presented here will go further along this path. The importance of longitudinal experiences is also being recognised by researchers, and here again, this analysis has a unique contribution to offer.

In the account of women's experiences which follows, it is recognised that certain ambiguity now attaches to the term 'career' because the prescriptive use has come to dominate. In order to avoid ambiguity at this stage, the patterns of women's occupational experiences which are described below are referred to as 'profiles'; the term has been described elsewhere as one of a set of concepts for handling work history data (Dex, 1984a). The term 'profile' is intended to be a wholly descriptive concept of experiences over time.

It is interesting that at least one commentator on work history experiences doubts whether it is even possible to construct occupational profiles for the population at large; possibly he means for men.[2]

APPROACHING THE WES DATA

An inspection of individual women's occupational histories was carried out using women's recorded occupational status from the point of leaving school until 1980 and their reasons for leaving jobs, in the context of women's other life and family events. Occupations had been classified in WES using a 12-fold set of categories which are listed in Table 3.1 on p. 38.[3] Several categories were later found to be too broad. The clerical category (5) includes both secretaries and lower grade clerical work; the nursing category (3) includes both trained nurses and nursing auxiliaries.

In a sense these categories set a limit to the occupational movements which we can see in these data; if we had a larger number of categories we might be able to see more movements between them, movements which take place within one category of this smaller set. Since we are hoping to identify patterns of occupational movements it could be argued that the patterns are therefore dependent on the set of occupational categories used. One way of testing whether any identified patterns are artefacts of the categories or whether they reflect women's experiences is to see if examples can be found of each pattern in other sources; for example, in case studies.

A set of profiles were found from an inspection of a sample of these women of different ages. A computer program was devised to identify these types and an attempt was made to classify all women in the data by running the program on the whole sample. This procedure acts as a test of the accuracy of the typology and the first run left 305 of the 5320 women unclassifiable. A further inspection of these cases led to some modification of the categories and ultimately a small number had to be classified in a miscellaneous category.

One further issue which has to be resolved before the classification of these women can take place is how much of the women's occupational history should we include when making the classification and assigning them to one of the types of profile. Women's experiences might well receive a different classification if only their first two jobs were used to make the classification from that which would emerge if their whole life's work was included. It may only be the frequencies of the categories which vary, however, and not their nature. This issue was resolved by first giving the frequencies of each profile based on women's experiences prior to childbirth, and then following these women's experiences through into later life. The occupational profiles described below do represent the whole of the work history experiences of some women, however. In the case of other women their profiles were disrupted at different points for various reasons which will be described.

OCCUPATIONAL PROFILES

A list of the most common profiles with a brief description is set out below along with the usual entry route into the profile; that is, the first job. The list excludes professionals since not only were women with professional occupations a very small group, hardly any women maintained a professional profile even prior to childbirth.

Teacher;	the woman has a succession of wholly teaching jobs after starting out with a teaching job. Women sometimes became teachers after starting out in professional occupations.
Nurse;	the woman has a succession of wholly nursing jobs after starting out with a nursing job. Women sometimes had teaching jobs in nursing later in their life.
Clerical;	the woman has a succession of wholly clerical jobs. The entry route was mostly by a clerical job but also by a brief semi-skilled job (including shop assistants).
Skilled;	the woman has a succession of skilled jobs and often will have a semi-skilled factory job during her profile. The entry route is most commonly a skilled job but can be a semi-skilled factory job.
Semi-skilled factory;	the woman has a succession of wholly semi-skilled factory jobs.
Semi-skilled;	the woman moves between semi-skilled jobs frequently; these include semi-skilled factory, child-care, shop assistant, semi-skilled domestic, other semi-skilled and sometimes clerical work (which is assumed to be low-grade clerical work). Entry to this profile can be via any of these occupations but 40 per cent of the profile had a first job as a shop assistant and many others started off in unskilled work.

Table 3.1   Occupational categories

1. *Professional occupations*
   Barristers, solicitors, chartered and certified accountants, university teachers, doctors, dentists, physicists, chemists, social scientists, pharmacists, dispensing opticians, qualified engineers, architects, town planners, civil servants – Assistant Secretary level and above.

2. *Teachers*
   Primary and secondary school teachers, teachers in further and higher education (not universities), head teachers, nursery teachers, vocational and industrial trainers.

3. *Nursing, medical and social occupations*
   SRN, SEN, nursing auxiliary, midwife, health visitor, children's nurse, matron/superintendent, dental nurse, dietician, radiographer, physiotherapist, chiropodist, dispenser, medical technician, houseparents, welfare occupations (including social workers), occupational therapist.

4. *Other intermediate non-manual occupations*
   Civil Servants – Executive Officer to Senior Principal level and equivalent in central and local government, computer programmer, systems analyst, O&M analyst, librarian, surveyor, personnel officer, managers, self-employed farmers, shopkeepers, publicans, hoteliers, buyers, company secretary, author, writer, journalist, artist, designer, window dresser, entertainer, musician, actress.

5. *Clerical occupations*
   Typist, secretary, shorthand writer, clerk, receptionist, personal assistant, cashier, (not retail), telephonist receptionist, office machine operator, computer operator, punch card operator, data processor, draughtswoman, tracer, market research interviewer, debt collector.

6. *Shop assistant and related sales occupations*
   People selling goods in wholesale or retail establishments, cashiers, in retail shops, check out and cash and wrap operators, petrol pump attendant, sales representative, demonstrator, theatre/cinema usherette, programme seller, insurance agent.

7. *Skilled occupations*
   Hairdresser, manicurist, beautician, make-up artist, cook, domestic and institution housekeeper, nursery nurse, travel stewardess, ambulance woman, van driver and deliveries, baker, weaver, knitter, mender, darner, tailoress and dressmaker (whole garment), clothing cutter, milliner, upholsterer, bookbinder, precision instrument maker and repairer, instrument assemblers, laboratory assistant, driving instructor, policewoman.

8. *Childcare occupations*
   Childminder, school meals and playgroup supervisor or leader, nanny,

Table 3.1 *contd.*   Occupational categories

---

au pair, people doing housework in addition to childcare (NB exclude nursing and teaching).

9. *Semi-skilled factory work*
   Assembler, packer, labeller, grader, sorter, inspector, machinist, machine operator, paper wrapping, filling or sealing containers, spinner, doubler, twister, winder, reeler.

10. *Semi-skilled domestic work*
    Waitress, barmaid, canteen assistant, people serving food at tables or counters, serving school meals, home help, care attendant, ward orderly, housemaid, domestic worker.

11. *Other semi-skilled occupations*
    Agricultural worker, groom, kennel maid, shelf filler, bus conductress, ticket collector, post woman, mail sorter, laundress, dry cleaner, presser, mail order and catalogue agent, market and street trader, collector saleswoman, traffic warden, telephone operator, photographer.

12. *Unskilled occupations*
    Cleaner, charwoman, kitchen hand, labourer, messenger.

Women were thought to be displaying clear preferences for all but the semi-skilled profile in that disruptions to the pattern were often followed by quick returns to it, and there is other evidence from case study material that these profiles describe genuine experiences. In this sense, many of the profiles constitute 'a career' for women in the sense that they exhibit attachment to certain occupations which they prefer and pursue. Stewart, Prandy and Blackburn's (1980) point about the unevenness of the occupational classification may not be so applicable to women's occupations since even semi-skilled women's occupations have longer term significance if they form part of an occupational profile.

DISRUPTIONS

Women experienced disruptions over their lifetime which often resulted in downward occupational mobility, although this was sometimes temporary with women returning to their former status. Getting married and moving, moving because of the husband's job, redundancies and dismissals were disruptions which women experienced before childbirth. Childbirth could sometimes be a disruption if it was unplanned but where women planned their childbirths, clearly they are not disruptions. Yeandle (1984) provides examples of both types. WES did not provide sufficient information to always distinguish those types. Childbirth could be a disruption when it occurred after women thought their families were complete; illness and redundancies were also common disruptions which often resulted in occupational downward mobility. The frequencies of the most common disruptions were linked to the type of profile in ways which we might expect; so that disruptions because of a husband's job were more likely to occur to women in teaching or nursing profiles, and illness and redundancy were more likely to occur to women in semi-skilled factory or skilled profiles. When disruptions occurred prior to a woman's first childbirth, their frequency of occurrence is recorded below.

FREQUENCIES OF PROFILES

How many women had these various patterns of occupational experiences? All the women in the sample who had ever worked were classified into one of the profiles. The 66 women left over after this classification was carried out were allocated to a Miscellaneous group. The frequencies of these various types of experiences were calculated (Table 3.2) firstly for women with children on the basis of their occupations up until childbirth (Column 1). Childless women were allocated to the profile categories on the basis of all of their recorded occupations (Column 2).

The two most frequently occurring profiles were semi-skilled (40 per cent) and clerical work (28 per cent). These two profiles also dominate the two sub-groups of women with children and childless women, who both have a large proportion of semi-skilled profiles (38–40 per cent). Childless women have a far higher proportion – 37 per cent – of clerical profiles; women with children have only 26 per cent in clerical profiles. This could mean that the incomplete early profiles of childless women mean that we are not yet able to classify them accurately and that fewer wholly clerical profiles will finally result, or that clerical work has been on the increase and this is

Table 3.2   Occupational profiles – per cent

Occupational profile	(1) Women with children*	(2) Childless women under age 40†	(3) Total
Professional	1	1	1
Semi-professional	9	13	10
Clerical	26	37	28
Skilled	5	5	5
Semi-skilled factory	16	6	14
Semi-skilled	40	38	40
Miscellaneous	1	1	1
No work before 1st birth	2	–	1
Total	100	100	100
$N =$	3922	1030	4952
Never worked	83	–	83
Childless Workers over 40 years	–	285	285
$N =$	4005	1315	5320

*Based on record of occupations prior to first childbirth.
†Based on record of all occupations up to 1980.

reflected in these younger childless women's experiences. There is probably something of both of these mechanisms at work here, but we cannot distinguish their quantitative significance. In addition, childless women have far fewer semi-skilled factory profiles which is probably a feature of their younger age distribution and the fact that manufacturing has been steadily declining in the post-war period. The childless (and younger) women also have more semi-professional profiles which again is what we would expect given the changes in education and the increases in job opportunities in these fields.

An age breakdown of the various profiles is given in Table 3.3. There are some variations across the age bands although the overall structure, with semi-skilled and clerical profiles predominating,

Table 3.3   Occupational profiles by age at interview (%)

Occupational profile	16–19	20–29	30–39	40–49	50–59
Professional	–	1	1	1	*
Semi-professional	5	12	13	9	6
Clerical	34	30	32	27	18
Skilled	6	5	6	5	4
Semi-skilled factory	14	10	12	16	18
Semi-skilled	40	39	34	39	50
Miscellaneous	1	2	1	1	1
No work before 1st birth	*	1	1	2	2
Total	100	100	100	100	100
N =	303	1232	1410	1003	1004

*Very low percentage.

remains. The over-50s age group have presumably been affected by their experiences during the war and that is the most likely explanation for the very high semi-skilled and semi-skilled factory profiles in this age group and the very low proportion of clerical profiles. The fact that the youngest age group's experiences are likely to be incomplete over their initial work phase and do not contain very many semi-professional profiles because they are too young makes generational trends more difficult to discern. Given these qualifications, semi-skilled profiles appear to have remained fairly constant in size, clerical profiles have increased slightly, semi-skilled factory profiles have been declining slightly and skilled profiles have stayed fairly constant.

It is possible to break down these total frequencies further; some women had a different starting point to their profile from that which was most common and there were varying amounts of mobility between the occupational categories as we shall see if we consider each profile separately.

PROFESSIONALS

A very small number of women in this sample experienced a

professional job over their work history; 33 (0.6 per cent of total sample) entered a professional job and another 19 had a professional job at some point during their working experience. An even smaller number of these women experienced anything which could be called a professional profile or career and the experience of these 52 women was very varied, more difficult to describe and much more unstable and unpredictable. In theory, this occupation need not be tied to any particular industry, but in practice, in the most consistent professional profiles, the professional jobs were in the professional and scientific industries.

A successful professional profile was one which had a succession of professional jobs, retaining occupational attachment over the whole or most of the work history. This only occurred in the cases where women were continuously employed, either because they were single and childless or because they took maternity leave instead of having breaks from work for childbirth. Most professional profiles were highly mobile between professional jobs and breaks for childbirth were often a smaller proportion of total job changing reasons; (there were several who stayed in one job for lengthy periods, however, just to illustrate the wide variety).

Entry into a professional profile was most commonly at the beginning of the work history as the first job or occasionally after a very short temporary job in a semi-skilled occupation, possibly to fill in waiting time. Another common route into a professional profile was through a clerical job of short duration with subsequent changes being between professional jobs. The third route into a professional job, but not into a professional profile, was to gain promotion with the same employer after a long and continued attachment to either clerical work, or clerical and intermediate non-manual work. This was rare.

As a group, professionals shared characteristics with teachers; they were older when they started work, more highly educated, occasionally married at the start of their work history and more likely to be under 40 years of age at the time of the survey. Many of those who started out in professional jobs at the beginning of their work histories did not continue in them for long. This disruption of moving-because-of-husband's-job was the main work disruption and it was experienced frequently during the initial work period. The loss of professional status was common after such a disruption and these women then moved into teaching, other intermediate non-manual and clerical jobs; this was downward occupational mobility. When teaching was the destination a teacher's profile then emerged but the other subsequent profiles were more varied. Redundancy was rare from professional jobs and only occurred in one case; a short shop assistant job then followed.

There were other pitfalls which occurred to those who maintained a full-time professional profile for some of their work history. In three cases women worked continuously over their childbirth period (taking maternity leave to have between 2 and 4 children), but a short time after their last birth they then left work because of illness and to look after their children and only one returned much later (after 12 years). This may have been a consequence of the strains of dual career families documented elsewhere.

Other disruptions to professional profiles came from voluntary job-changing through dissatisfaction, from leaving jobs to take up other education opportunities and from temporary professional jobs coming to an end. This set of events occurred often enough to illustrate that women who set out in professional jobs are less conventional in occupational attachment than other women and possibly more flexible with a wider set of options. They are also more used to temporary jobs and are less disrupted by them. There are however, very few cases from which to generalise and no information is available about how far the unsuccessful professional women regretted their status.

The return to work after childbirth was more likely to be in part-time work by a ratio of 3 to 1, even after maternity leave, and two-thirds of the part-time jobs were professional jobs. Thus whilst a professional status was difficult for women to maintain, it was not particularly because of the lack of part-time professional jobs for married women with children. Professionals despite their small numbers were an interesting and very varied group, on the increase in the post-war period, and in terms of their occupational attachment and industrial and job mobility, they were most like the semi-skilled profile group, although presumably better paid at least for some of their working lives.

SEMI-PROFESSIONAL PROFILES

These profiles all exhibited a high degree of occupational commitment so that women changed their jobs into others of the same kind. The commitment was similar to that visible in clerical profiles, the major difference being that teaching and nursing profiles were more successful at retaining their occupational status throughout their work histories. Involuntary job separations were far less frequent in these public sector occupations during the period covered by the survey;[4] movement between jobs was less than occurred in other occupations, especially for teachers, and work disruptions as a whole, when they did occur, resulted far less frequently in any occupational change, presumably because demand has been high fairly consistently. The occupational-industrial overlap thus played a crucial role in producing persistent teachers' and nurses' occupational profiles. Intermediate non-manual occupations, on the other hand, could be in the whole range of industries and their spread of job leaving reasons reflected this; there were more redundancies and dismissals, and a smaller proportion retained their occupational status throughout. In a few cases, women moved between teaching and intermediate non-manual jobs; (in this case they were classified according to which occupation they spent most of their time in).

The entry into these jobs, as with professionals, was, on the whole, at a later age (21 plus) than the other profiles and concomitantly with more education, although nurses were the exception in that they could start nursing at 17 or 18. This delay meant that the sequence of events over the initial work period could differ markedly from other women in that teachers etc. could be married before having any work experience – although this was not common. Whereas teachers had one main entry route into teaching after leaving full-time education, nursing and intermediate non-manual jobs had alternative routes, for example, from clerical profiles or from childcare and semi-skilled for nursing. Entry at the first job was the dominant route for all, however. When nursing or intermediate non-manual work was obtained later in the work history, it could be lost subsequently more easily than in other cases.

After entry into a nursing occupation, job changing was common, for three main reasons: because jobs were temporary; leaving to take-up education in nursing, usually linked to another nursing job; and because of the disruption to work of moving because of husband's job. The first two job-changing reasons were specific to nursing and are presumably caused by the structure and organisation of nurses' training. Both reasons were much less frequent in the later work cycles of these women.

Nursing was the one semi-professional occupational profile where it was possible to have more than one occupation legitimately in the profile; nurses could sometimes be promoted to nursing teachers and they also move between nursing and child-care occupations. In their later work cycle nurses also moved between nursing jobs in the public and private sector industries to a greater degree.

One feature which these semi-professional profiles shared was the dominance of 'moving because of husband' as a work disruption. It occurred frequently in these profiles and, presumably, it reflects greater geographical mobility of the husbands of the women in these occupations. It was very common for teachers to have two jobs during their initial work period, the first one ending because of moving with her husband's job; this reason for giving up a teaching job then recurred in the later working profile. A period of unemployment sometimes followed one of these disruptions with another teaching job being taken up later. This may be an indication that women from semi-professional profiles were less prepared to work in downwardly mobile occupations after a disruption and they would wait for a suitable job in preference. Household income levels presumably play a big role here. Married teachers occasionally switched from full-time to part-time work during the initial work period after a disruption to their work.

Downward occupational mobility, whilst not so frequent, did occur from semi-professional jobs after disruptions or breaks for childbirth. The destination occupations were as follows: teachers could end up in skilled or any of the semi-skilled occupations; intermediate non-manual workers went into clerical, shop assistant, or semi-skilled domestic jobs. Interestingly, teachers were the only occupational group not to have shop assistant jobs after breaks for childbirth or after disruptions to work.

The common transition from full-time to part-time work occurred in all the semi-professional profiles across the first childbirth break. Of the teachers who remained in teaching, over half were in part-time jobs on returning; nurses who retained their occupational status across this boundary were more likely to be in part-time jobs; over two-thirds worked part-time. This is by far the largest proportion of part-time work in the same occupation which suggests there is more opportunity for part-time work in nursing. The higher degree of occupational attachment of these groups across childbirth breaks also appears to be linked to their higher take-up of maternity leave.

Table 3.4 lists the frequencies of these semi-professional occupational profiles in the Women and Employment Survey; they are all minority groups. As the figures show, semi-professional profiles constitute approximately ten per cent of this sample; teachers' profiles are four per cent and nurses' five per cent. The other intermediate

Table 3.4   Semi-professional profiles before childbirth

	Number*	Percentage of total sample (N = 4952)
Teachers	189	3.8
Nurses	266	5.4
Other intermediate non manual	44	1.0
Disrupted intermediate non manual	5	

*Figures do not include those who achieved this occupational status by upward mobility from another profile.

non-manual profiles are the smallest group. (These figures do not include the full extent of the experiences of either teaching or nursing by women in this sample). Teaching within a predominantly nursing profile was counted as nursing and where it occurred as one job amidst others, as with semi-skilled jobs, it was not recognised as semi-professional teaching since the women concerned had few if any educational qualifications. Some professionals became teachers but they were included in the professional profile.

The age distribution of all three semi-professional profiles shows the same trend. There are very few of the older women (over 40) in these occupations and an increase throughout the post-war period. The figures suggest that there was a sharp increase in recruitment into these occupations.

CLERICAL PROFILES

A clerical occupational profile is one in which a woman has a succession of clerical jobs and only clerical jobs throughout her work history. Departures from clerical jobs could occur when women experienced disruptions to their work, described in more detail later, or over breaks for childbirth. Women who had set out on this type of occupational path on leaving school exhibited a strong commitment to it, and often returned to a clerical job shortly after the experience of an interim non-clerical job which followed disruptions to work. This commitment to clerical work was seen to operate despite work interruptions and across work cycle boundaries where periods of not working to have childbirths occurred. It was also a profile exhibited by continuous workers. In this way, it could be labelled 'a pure career' since the commitment implies a conscious preference for and pursuit of clerical jobs. A clerical profile did not entail any commitment to a single industry or a type of industry but is clearly an industry-mobile skill which transcends industry boundaries.

The most common route into a clerical profile occurred through getting a clerical job on leaving school, although there was another minor route of first having a semi-skilled job and moving fairly quickly into clerical work and then staying there. In a very small number of cases (four in all) a clerical profile was preceded by a job in nursing or the skilled occupational category. When entry into clerical work occurred immediately on leaving school one of two types of experiences followed.

A *stable start* clerical profile occurred when a woman had only one clerical job over the whole of the initial work period, or in the case of continuous workers, women spent approximately ten years or more in their first clerical job. The alternative was a *mobile* clerical profile when a woman had a succession of clerical jobs over the initial work period and left one clerical job voluntarily to take up another. Most commonly jobs were given up because the women were dissatisfied or had a better job to go to. These two types of clerical profile merged into one through the later phases of the work cycle, as women changed their jobs as a consequence of stopping work to have children.

Whilst these two main types have been identified, it should be noted that there was a group of women who had two clerical jobs during the initial work period, and in some of these cases the first job was very short. Where the first job was of a very short duration, the group shared things in common with the stable start workers, namely a shorter initial work period duration. In the other cases their characteristics are similar to the mobile group and on the whole it seemed best to incorporate this group with the mobile clerical profiles when relationships with other variables are discussed later.

The other minor route into a clerical profile was to start off in semi-skilled work and move after one or two jobs at the most, because of dissatisfaction/better job into clerical work – thereafter pursuing a mobile clerical profile. It may have been the case that these women wanted, but were unable to get clerical jobs when they left school, but did not give up. The tenacity with which they, like other clerical workers, then stayed in clerical occupations is again an indication of a commitment and conscious preference for clerical work over the semi-skilled and usually manual occupations. This is one case of relative upward occupational mobility although it occurs from a semi-skilled start and is discussed more fully under that heading.

Clerical profiles like all occupational profiles could be disrupted by a series of circumstances; namely, redundancy or dismissal, moving at marriage or after marriage because of the husband's job, or because of illness. Illness occurred infrequently as a disruption to work, but moving because of one's husband was very important in this and other non-manual jobs. It was not very important in the manual and semi-skilled profiles. This perhaps indicates that these clerical profile women were married to geographically more mobile husbands.

When one of these disruptions ended the first job, as in 196 cases, the effect was to turn a potentially stable start profile either into a mobile clerical profile, or to disrupt the clerical profile. The disruption could either be temporary, if the woman was able later to get another clerical job, or in some cases the disruption was permanent and she then followed an alternative. Thus downward occupational mobility could occur as a result of one of these disruptions. Of the 196 women whose first job in clerical work was disrupted, 92 (47 per cent) recovered their clerical profile status before their first childbirth; the rest experienced downward mobility, into a semi-skilled profile (described below). The main destination occupations which women could move to from a clerical profile were shop assistants and semi-skilled domestic work. Women could also have this experience of downward occupational mobility over their breaks from work for childbirth.

Of those who started out in clerical profiles, over 50 per cent were still in clerical jobs in their final working period,[5] although there were many who were not in clerical jobs later on, most of whom had experienced downward occupational mobility. Mobile clerical workers were more successful in staying in clerical work, despite disruptions and births, than were stable start clerical workers. Possibly they were more ambitious and certainly they were more experienced in job search and job changing, and had longer durations of working prior to childbirth.

Upward mobility was less common although it did occur mainly into the category called 'other intermediate non-manual' or into nursing and very occasionally into professional occupations. Becoming a supervisor within the clerical occupation was more common. Being a continuous worker, with no children, improved a woman's chance of upward mobility from a clerical profile but even then it was still infrequent, and in many cases it was a temporary move to be followed shortly after by a move back into clerical work.

Where a clerical profile was maintained across the first childbirth break from work, the job after childbirth could be part-time clerical work, and was more likely to be in part-time clerical work by a two to one ratio. A move into part-time work over childbirth was common for all women, but of the clerical workers who made this transition, 54 per cent took up part-time jobs in other occupations, whereas only 28 per cent of those taking full-time jobs over this boundary lost their clerical status.

A brief summary of the frequencies of some of these different types of clerical profile in the Women and Employment Survey are displayed in Table 3.5. The distinction between the various clerical profiles was made on the basis of their experiences before childbirth

Table 3.5   Clerical profiles up to childbirth

	Number	Percentage of total sample (N = 4952)*
Stable start clerical	455	9.2
Mobile clerical	638	12.9
Disrupted – 1st job clerical	196	4.0
Recovers profile after disruption	92	1.9
Clerical profile after semi-skilled start	85	1.7
Clercial profile from other occupation start	4	†
Total clerical profile‡	1274	25.7
Potential clerical profile§	1378	

*Total sample = 4952 cases which excludes 83 cases who have no work experience and 285 women over 40 who had no children at the interview.
†Very low percentage.
‡Includes all above items with exception of 196 disrupted.
§Includes disrupted cases.

since later they merge into one type. The total shows the frequency of actual clerical profiles in this sample and the potential clerical profiles. As the figures show, clerical profiles are very common amongst the women in this survey. The vast majority of those with this type of profile at least at the beginning of their work history were aged between 20 and 45 at the time of the survey which means that they started work between 1950 and 1975. According to other commentators these were largely the days of the seller's market for clerical skills (McNally, 1979, p. 91 cites Fulop). Interestingly, and perhaps not unexpectedly, those who experienced a disruption to their first clerical job were more frequently in the younger age group starting work after 1970, when the market was not so favourable.

Further support for the existence of clerical profiles, their poor promotion possibilities and their attraction over and above manual work can be found in studies by Crompton, Jones and Reid (1982), McNally (1979) and Silverstone (1974 and 1975).

SKILLED PROFILES

A skilled profile is relatively rare. Where it occurs, a commitment to skilled work is visible. This profile very largely resembles that of the semi-skilled factory profile since they are both in manual occupations and it might be more appropriate to aggregate these two groups. Skilled jobs were held with a very low frequency by women in this survey. The low frequency of skilled profiles is not an indicator that skilled jobs are more likely to be found in conjunction with other occupations than on their own; they are just not very likely to be found at all. (Having said that a large proportion of the unclassified profiles described at the end contain skilled jobs – but in total, these are a very small number).

A skilled profile could start with one skilled job after leaving school until the first childbirth, a *stable start skilled* profile. Alternatively, a succession of skilled jobs could follow the first job before the first childbirth; a *mobile skilled profile*. These two experiences occurred with almost similar frequencies.

A disruption followed the first skilled job in 84 cases and these workers could then experience downward occupational mobility into semi-skilled, unskilled or shop assistant jobs. In some cases women later recovered their skilled status (21 cases or 25 per cent) but in others (75 per cent) their occupational profile changed and became more like a semi-skilled profile (as described below). Downward occupational mobility could also occur over the first break for childbirth and skilled workers also entered part-time work on their return to work after childbirth. A higher proportion of this small group of skilled profile women workers than was the case with the semi-skilled factory profiles, retained their skilled status over this break for childbirth; possibly this was because more of them went back to full-time skilled work than was the case in the semi-skilled factory profiles. In other respects skilled profiles were very similar to semi-skilled factory profiles. The frequencies of this small group are listed in Table 3.6. Women with skilled profiles constituted only four per cent of this sample.

Table 3.6   Skilled profiles before childbirth

	Number	Percentage of the total sample (N = 4952)
Stable start skilled	79	1.6
Mobile skilled	95	1.9
Disrupted 1st job skilled	84	1.7
Recovered skilled status (Before childbirth)	21	0.4
Total*	195	3.9
Potential skilled profiles†	258	

*Includes all above except 84 disrupted.
†Includes disrupted cases.

SEMI-SKILLED FACTORY PROFILES

This profile exhibits the sort of commitment to semi-skilled factory work that was visible in the clerical profiles. Jobs in semi-skilled factory work were taken up after disruptions to work, after breaks for childbirth and after short spells in other occupations which sometimes followed either of the other events, in the process breaking the continuity of the profile. Whilst the commitment to the occupation appeared to be similar to that of clerical workers, and in that sense a semi-skilled factory profile constituted a pure career, consciously pursued and chosen in preference to others, the origin of the commitment may be different. Semi-skilled factory profiles were specific to manufacturing industries and in some cases, they were specific to single manufacturing industries, in particular to textiles.[6] It could be the case that local labour market constraints played a more influential role in the formation of semi-skilled factory profiles than they did for clerical profiles, although an element of choice and preference by the workers clearly remained. Even in an area where semi-skilled factory jobs are the predominant employment for women, there are still likely to be a range of shop assistant and clerical jobs.

The main gateway into a semi-skilled factory profile was through getting a semi-skilled factory job as the first job after leaving school; then one of two types could follow. A *stable start* semi-skilled factory profile occurred when a woman had only one job in this occupation, in a manufacturing industry, up to the first childbirth. (The vast majority of women with only one job over this period were in the two occupations of clerical and semi-skilled factory work). A *mobile* semi-skilled factory profile was one where two or more jobs in semi-skilled factory work were held before childbirth. The two types merged together to form a mobile profile over the later stages of the work cycle. There were two kinds of mobile semi-skilled factory profiles; one which was industry specific, usually in textiles, and, in the other, job changes were across the four manufacturing industries classified in this survey. It does not seem unreasonable to suppose that the industry specific semi-skilled factory profile arose out of the dominance of that industry in local labour markets, although this cannot be investigated with these data. Similar constraints may also have been operating on the semi-skilled factory profiles with a stable start. In fact, where the more complete work histories were available for older women, industry specific semi-skilled factory jobs in textiles often followed in the later work periods after a stable start in textiles, which is some support for this idea.

Disruptions to work occurred during the working lives of women with semi-skilled factory profiles. Redundancies and dismissals constituted a much larger proportion of disruptions to semi-skilled factory (and skilled work) than they did to clerical work. Moving at marriage was another important disruption but moving because of husband's job, subsequent to marriage, was a far less significant work disruption for this group. These women may be married to men who had more locally based, possibly manual jobs. Illness also occurred to disrupt work and although it was a more minor reason for changing jobs, it occurred more frequently to semi-skilled factory workers than it did to clerical workers; perhaps this is a concomitant part of physically demanding work. A disruption caused the first semi-skilled factory job to end in 145 cases (three per cent of the total sample) and as a result many of these workers experienced either a semi-skilled factory mobile profile or downward occupational mobility if they were not so lucky. The downward occupational mobility was temporary in some cases when further semi-skilled factory jobs followed later, but permanent in others. Only 27 per cent of the 145 women whose first semi-skilled factory job was disrupted managed to retain or recover their status in a semi-skilled factory profile before their first childbirth. When they did not recover their status their profile changed to a semi-skilled profile.

Downward occupational mobility occurred from a semi-skilled factory profile after disruptions and after breaks for childbirth. The downwardly mobile destination occupations from this semi-skilled factory origin were semi-skilled domestic work, unskilled work and to a lesser extent, shop assistants. In two of these cases the mobility meant a transition from manufacturing to service industries.

Upward occupational mobility was again rare and where it occurred it was into skilled jobs in the same industry, or becoming a supervisor also in the same industry or with the same employer. Such moves were usually temporary and returns to semi-skilled factory work followed.

The first break from work for childbirth was also a transition from full-time to part-time work for a semi-skilled factory profile in a similar ratio to the clerical profiles; two to one in favour of part-time work. In general, a higher proportion retained jobs in semi-skilled factory work after this break but these were predominantly women who took up full-time jobs after childbirth; 78 per cent of the full-time post-birth jobs of this group who had started out in semi-skilled factory profiles were still in semi-skilled factory work but only 42 per cent of the part-time jobs were in semi-skilled factory jobs. This loss of semi-skilled factory status did not prevent these women from returning to this occupation at a later date, however.

A summary of the frequencies of semi-skilled factory profiles in this sample is set out in Table 3.7, again based on the period before childbirth. Semi-skilled factory profiles account for a sizeable proportion of the experiences of women in this sample, 11 per cent

Table 3.7 Semi-skilled factory profile up to childbirth

	Number	Percentage of the total sample (N = 4952)
Stable start semi-skilled factory	248	5.0
Mobile semi-skilled factory	281	5.7
Disrupted 1st job	145	2.9
Recovers semi-skilled factory status (prior to childbirth)	39	6.8
Total semi-skilled factory*	568	11.5
Potential semi-skilled profiles†	674	

*Includes all above items with exception of 145 disrupted.
†Includes disrupted cases.

altogether, although this is smaller than the clerical profile group. The age distribution of semi-skilled factory profiles documented later reveals that there is a marked decline in moving from older women where this experience constitutes approximately 15 per cent of the sample of oldest women (50–59 at the survey), to 10 per cent in the younger age group (16–30). These figures suggest that the entry into semi-skilled factory profiles has been declining steadily in the post-Second World War period. Since this occupational profile is wholly in the manufacturing industries, and often in textiles, this is a general reflection of the steady decline in British textiles and manufacturing industries as a whole. The frequencies of women's occupational profile experiences are strongly related to general trends in the economic structure – especially as in the case of textiles where women are a large proportion of the workforce of that industry. In this sample, the deindustrialisation of the British economy is reducing the opportunities for women to pursue semi-skilled factory profiles.

Further support for the existence of semi-skilled factory profiles, their poor promotion prospects and the lower than average availability of part-time work can be found in Coyle's (1982) work on the clothing manufacturing industry (which would have been classified as textiles in this WES survey), and Cavendish's (1982) account of assembly work.[7] The continual employment of women in these jobs throughout their work history is attributed to negative recruitment policies by Coyle's sources; employers have not tried to persuade older married women to enter the industry for the first time which some say is because of a 'mental block' (Coyle, 1982, p. 17) although there may be other rational considerations if part-time work is not favoured and the textile industry as a whole relies on immigrant labour power.

SEMI-SKILLED PROFILE

In this profile, a woman moves between semi-skilled jobs fairly frequently over the initial work period and subsequently. There was little evidence of any attachment to a single occupation since movement took place mainly between shop assistant, semi-skilled factory, other semi-skilled work, semi-skilled domestic jobs and more occasionally clerical work.[8] Childcare occupations were also included in this list although jobs in this occupation were rare. A semi-skilled profile is therefore inherently mobile in character, and moves between industries occurred frequently.

A semi-skilled profile was a commonly-experienced occupational profile. Entry into it was often (40 per cent of cases) by a shop assistant job on leaving school – which was held for a very short duration before moving on to another semi-skilled job. The size of this group meant that a large proportion of women leaving school entered into shop assistant work but rarely did they stay in it. There were only a small number of women who stayed in shop assistants' jobs up to their first childbirth. Shop assistant jobs recurred over the rest of this semi-skilled profile but they were often short in duration and women usually left because of dissatisfaction or having a better job. Shop assistant jobs, whilst frequently held by women, constituted one of the most mobile occupations; they were either part of this mobile semi-skilled profile, or they were temporary downwardly mobile destination occupations from other profiles. (A small number of cases did have a succession of solely shop assistant jobs over their initial work period and these are included in Table 3.8). These results seem to locate shop assistant work firmly in the semi-skilled manual category – and not alongside non-manual women's work.

Another route into a semi-skilled profile is through the first job or

Table 3.8   Semi-skilled and associated profiles up to childbirth

	Number	Percentage of total sample (N = 4952)
Semi-skilled profile	1621	32.7
Semi-skilled after unskilled start	88	1.8
Shop assistant only	256	5.2
Total semi-skilled	1965	39.7

even two jobs being in unskilled work in any of the manufacturing or service industries. After a very short duration in unskilled work, the woman moved into some sort of semi-skilled work and then continued along a semi-skilled occupational profile as described above. This is not the only outcome to an unskilled start, but it is the most common. Unskilled work for women appeared to be the most highly mobile occupational category. Few women stayed in this category for any length of time and since it is at the bottom of the status hierarchy, upward vertical mobility took place through moving out of unskilled work. There were no wholly unskilled occupational profiles. Given the actual movement out of unskilled work, it would seem to suggest that it is the least preferred type of women's work, sometimes taken up only after a period of initial unemployment.

Many of those who started off in unskilled work but moved into semi-skilled profiles subsequently, shared the characteristics of a semi-skilled profile, as described above; in this sense they may constitute a sub-group: the unskilled start. As a sub-group of semi-skilled profiles, the unskilled start had much more job mobility over the initial work period up to childbirth, and they were more likely to move back into unskilled work at some time later in the work cycle.

Disruptions occurred within the semi-skilled profile of similar types and proportions to those in the semi-skilled factory profile; redundancies and dismissals, and moving at marriage were common. Less frequent were moving because of husband's jobs and illness, although in the case of illness it was a more frequent occurrence than in non-manual occupational profiles. The consequences of disruptions, however, were less distinctive since in the majority of cases, the occupation which followed was one of those already experienced at an earlier point in the profile. In this sense, downward mobility is difficult to discern. Downward mobility probably did occur however after disruptions or breaks for childbirth, into unskilled work, although women rarely stayed for long in unskilled work, as mentioned earlier. The move into unskilled work was more likely to occur if women had started out in unskilled work.

Upward occupational mobility was more common out of a semi-skilled profile and women moved into mobile clerical work from this start, usually towards the end of their initial work period before childbirth. The break for childbirth sometimes meant that the higher status was not maintained into the later working profile although it was for some. It is possible that some of this seemingly upward mobility into clerical work is spurious and is instead horizontal mobility to low level clerical jobs. Some movements from semi-skilled to nursing occupations were thought likely to be of this nature and related to the anomalies of the occupational classification.

Over the first break for childbirth a similar transition by two-thirds of these women into part-time work took place; this is the same ratio of part-time to full-time experienced by other occupational groups. The part-time work was more likely to be in semi-skilled domestic work although large proportions were also in shop assistant, semi-skilled factory and unskilled jobs. Full-time jobs, on the other hand, were far more likely to be in semi-skilled factory jobs.

The frequencies of the semi-skilled profile in this sample are listed in Table 3.8. This is the largest single profile group representing 40 per cent of these women. Those who started out on a semi-skilled profile were distributed in varying proportions across the age groups with a bulge at either end; the over 50s and the under 20s had approximately 36 per cent and 30 per cent in this occupational profile in comparison to figures around 20 per cent in the other age groups although the trend seemed to be for a steady increase of these occupational profiles since 1955.

The women who entered the semi-skilled profile through unskilled work differed, however. Over half of this group were over 50 years at the time of the survey and the frequencies decline markedly in moving to the younger age groups. Some of this age trend reflects a feature of the coding scheme but some of the result suggests that unskilled jobs for women have been on the decline in the post-war period. Unskilled jobs appear to be last-resort jobs which women have either taken at the beginning of their work histories or later, when nothing better was available; then movement out to another job was effected as soon as possible.

MISCELLANEOUS PROFILES

There were 66 women whose occupational profiles were difficult to classify. They are obviously in the minority, constituting approximately one per cent of this sample but they all share a common occupational experience; they at some time experienced a skilled occupation. Broadly speaking they fall into three types. Firstly, some women experienced a combination of skilled and semi-skilled factory jobs over their initial work phase (12 women in all). It is possible that this experience was similar to that of a semi-skilled factory profile but it is difficult to be sure. The second group (33 women) had a mixture of skilled jobs, clerical and nursing jobs most often starting off their profile, after leaving school, with a skilled job. The third group (21 women) had a skilled job as their first job after leaving school but then had a succession of semi-skilled jobs with an occasional skilled job interspersed with what in other respects appeared to be a semi-skilled profile. These profiles may be genuine minority experiences of women, but alternatively they may have more in common with the major profiles described earlier and only appear different because of inadequacies in the occupational classification. It is not possible to be more specific here so that these groups have been left under the heading miscellaneous.

WOMEN'S EDUCATIONAL QUALIFICATIONS

The highest educational qualifications of these women on leaving school are cross-tabulated with their occupational profiles in Table 3.9. There are some clear associations in the table. Women who left school without any qualifications are highly likely to have a semi-skilled or a semi-skilled factory profile; together these groups account for 77 per cent of the groups of women with the lowest education. At the other end of the education spectrum, women who left school with an A level or above were highly likely to have one of the semi-professional profiles (51 per cent), the non-manual profiles together account for 72 per cent of this group of women. Perhaps it is worth noting here that, despite having an A level, 23 per cent of these women still have a

Table 3.9   Occupational profiles by women's highest educational qualifications on leaving school (%)

Occupational profile	No qualifications	CSE (not gd. 1) clerical trade apprentice	O level CSE (gd. 1) City & Guilds	A level or above
Professional	*	–	*	4
Semi-professional	1	1	3	51
Clerical	14	52	55	17
Skilled	1	8	3	3
Semi-skilled factory	25	5	1	*
Semi-skilled	52	32	28	23
Miscellaneous	1	2	1	1
No work before 1st birth	2	1	1	1
Total	100	100	100	100
N	2486	702	945	819

*Less than 0.5%.

semi-skilled profile although none of them has a semi-skilled factory profile.

The groups of women with some qualifications were similar to each other and quite distinct from the other two groups. Women with some qualifications seem highly likely to have a clerical profile (52–55 per cent); the next highest frequency is the semi-skilled profile (28–32 per cent) and these two profiles, which were the most predominant in the whole sample, constitute 83–84 per cent of these cases.

These results probably confirm what we would expect; that there is a strong overlap between women's occupational and educational experiences. Women who have non-manual occupations and, in particular here, non-manual occupational profiles, are those who leave school with some educational qualifications; women who have no qualifications are more likely to be in semi-skilled and manual profiles and women with higher education qualifications take up semi-professional profiles. Education is likely to be a reasonable predictor of women's occupational experiences up to childbirth. In this sense, the attention Crompton and Sanderson (1985) have drawn to the phenomenal growth in women's educational credentials in recent years is worth noting; the implication is that women will start to break through more into the higher grade occupations. On the other hand, these figures show that there is a large amount of underachievement even at this early stage of women's careers. We would need more information about young women's subjective preferences for occupations in order to be sure that this was not 'chosen' underachievement. More limited studies suggest that there are significant mismatches between job aspirations and achievements (Dex, 1982; Coyle, 1984).[9] However, systematic research on strategies of occupational choice is sadly lacking.

The view of the operations of labour markets which these data suggest is one which sees a certain amount of slots allocated to young women and later older women. Women seeking jobs then queue up, so to speak, to fill the slots and those with higher education are at the front of the queue. Nonetheless the subjective elements of the allocation process whereby employers make decisions on the basis of personal preference, appearance etc., means that education will not be a wholly successful predictor for individuals of their occupational attainment, although it will have some influence. These themes are developed in more detail later.

HOUSEHOLD RELATIONSHIPS

How are women's occupational profiles related to their husband's employment? We have already noted that women can experience disruptions to their working lives; disruptions can start to occur when women get married if that involves moving a sufficient distance from their current job. Some women experienced the disruption of having to move subsequently because of their husband's job. Martin and Roberts (1984, table 7.14) show that 3 per cent of women who were not working in 1980 gave the reason for leaving their last job as 'moved because of husband's job'. This figure underestimates the percentage of women who have ever had this experience at some time in their working life. As we noted earlier, the frequency of the various types of disruption was related to women's type of occupational profile; disruptions because of a husband's job were far more likely to occur to women with teaching or nursing profiles. Women in these occupations seem more likely, therefore, to experience disruptions to their employment career from their husband's employment. We might expect to see the husbands of these women in different types of jobs; presumably the geographically mobile jobs.

A table setting out the relationship between women's occupational profiles and husband's employment in 1980 is provided in Table 3.10. These figures suggest that there is a tendency for women who have manual profiles to have husbands in manual jobs, and that husbands with non-manual occupations are more likely to have wives with non-manual occupational profiles, at least up to their first childbirth. We should remember here that we are comparing women's experiences at the beginning of their work cycle with their husband's job at the interview. These results do coincide with our expectations, however, since non-manual employment for men probably involves far more geographical mobility than manual work.

Whilst this association between husbands' occupations and women's occupational profiles exists, there are large numbers of cases where these experiences do not overlap. In the case of women with husbands in the highest SEG groups (1–4, 12 and 13), 31 per cent of the wives had a semi-skilled occupational profile and the percentages are similar or higher for the other non-manual categories of husband's employment. It is less surprising but worth noting that men in skilled manual or foremen's socio-economic groups regularly have wives in clerical (or other non-manual) profiles; up to as much as 30 per cent of cases. Men in semi-skilled and unskilled socio-economic groups are less likely to have wives with non-manual occupational profiles, but even there, as many as 21 per cent of semi-skilled workers' wives in this sample can be in non-manual occupational profiles.

We might ask whether the cases where women's occupations are seemingly higher than those of men's (if we rank non-manual work higher than manual), constitute cross-class families of the kind described by Heath and Britten (1984) and McRae (1986). If cross-class families exist on the scale suggested by these figures it would seriously question the appropriateness of using men's occupations to reflect the class category or status of families. This is what Britten and Heath (1984) argue to be the case. We must note, firstly, that the WES data do not provide information about men's occupations over time so that we cannot be sure that the occupations recorded in 1980 for these men reflect their lifetime class affiliation. Nonetheless many other studies have only had cross-sectional data of the same kind as a basis for theorising about men and class. Neither do we have here the problem that other studies have encountered, that women's sales work has been classified as non-manual when, in fact, it is quite

Table 3.10 Occupational profiles by husband's socio-economic group

Woman's Occupational profile	Husband's occupations (SEG) percentages (rounded) in each occupational profile							
	Employer Managers etc SEG 1–4, 12, 13	Intermediate non-manual SEG 5	Junior non-manual SEG 6	Foreman SEG 8	Skilled Manual SEG 9	Semi-skilled & personal service SEG 10, 7	Unskilled	Others
Professional	2	1	*	*	*	*	–	–
Semi-professional	16	26	8	5	5	5	1	10
Clerical	38	28	36	26	23	16	11	16
Skilled	4	6	6	5	5	6	4	5
Semi-skilled factory	7	4	10	16	19	25	28	17
Semi-skilled	31	29	38	46	44	44	53	50
Miscellaneous	1	5	1	1	1	1	1	–
No work before 1st birth	1	5	1	1	1	3	2	3
Total	100	100	100	100	100	100	100	100
N	1184	332	311	294	1041	432	125	151

Note: Sample is married women only where husband's SEG available.

low grade manual work. These WES data on women's occupations are still subject to a limitation, however; the clerical occupational categor contains a wide range of clerical jobs, some of which are likely to be o a very low level; for example, filing clerks.

Allowing for some overestimation in the figures, there are a sizeable number of families in Britain in 1980 where the woman was employee in non-manual clerical work and the man in manual work. We are unable to explore the consequences of this pattern. But it would appear to be a worthwhile topic of research to explore the life-style political allegiance, children's attainment and other potential differ ences of these households in comparison with those where husband and wife have similar occupations or where the husband has a bette occupation than the woman.[10] The fact that women's occupationa profiles fall into particular types means that women's intermitten employment will not cause them to be dropped from samples when such analyses are undertaken. More information is needed, therefore before we can be sure about the difference women's occupations make to households and their class. Ultimately, a series of empirica questions about the effect of women's employment on a whole range of household concerns remain to be asked and answered.

CONCLUSIONS

We can draw some preliminary conclusions from the analysis o women's work histories described in this chapter. A set of occupa tional profiles have been identified for women which describe most women's experiences for their whole working lives. These profiles enable us to infer that women have attachments to certain occupations (clerical, skilled, semi-skilled factory and semi-professionals) which persist through disruptions and voluntary breaks for childbirth. Women clearly distinguish between, and have preferences for, certain kinds of work especially since most job changing is voluntary. The persistence of these preferences over periods of childbirth and after disruptions makes it sensible to construct occupational profiles which cover the whole work history. Women's work experiences should not be seen as compartmentalised and their commitment to work should not be thought to be casual or purely demand-determined. In so far as these occupations are the consciously-pursued goals of women they constitute occupational careers (not solely in semi-professional or non-manual occupations).

Women's education on leaving school is in part a predictor of their occupational profile but there is room for underachievement to occur. The first job after leaving school is important although it is not completely determining of the occupational profile which follows. The first job will be a very good indicator of a profile if it is a semi-skilled job. The least preferred occupations with the highest turnover appear to be unskilled and shop assistant occupations. Shop assistant jobs appear to be filled mainly by school leavers who stay a very short time, or older women on their first return to work after childbirth.

The frequencies of occupational profiles in different age groups reflected macro trends which are known to have been occurring. Manufacturing-linked profiles can be seen to have been declining and public sector and services occupations have been on the increase in the younger women's experiences. The ability to identify patterns of women's occupational experiences over time offers the chance of providing a classification of their occupations even when they are not in employment. We must use this information carefully, however, as the results of the next chapter point out. A route is now available to explore more of the differences between households where men and women have different or similar occupational statuses. This sort of empirical work would be a foundation for a class analysis which integrates women and women's employment into accounts of the class structure; it would enable many more questions about household relations to be explored in the context of both women's and men's employment. The availability of men's employment histories would obviously be a valuable addition to such analyses.

4 Occupational Mobility

INTRODUCTION

An examination of the way women move between jobs was a central focus of the empirical analysis reported in the last chapter. The occupational profiles described there were constructed essentially from horizontal movements between occupation groups; that is between jobs which were in the same occupational category or an equivalent status occupation. When disruptions occurred to women' employment, vertical occupational mobility was found to occur in many instances; that is, movements up or down, but mainly down the occupational scale. It is to these vertical movements we now turn. The WES data provided the rare opportunity to examine women' experiences of vertical occupational mobility over their lifetime. The analysis rests, of course, on being able to identify vertical moves up and down the occupational scale; this is an issue which is discussed below. It was possible to see from the results when and why vertical occupational mobility occurred, the extent of these experiences and how often women recovered from a loss of occupational status. The findings have an important bearing on the theories of labour market mechanisms and how women fit into labour market structures.

There are a growing number of studies of women's occupational mobility. Many of the studies have used large-scale data and aggregate analyses from which conclusions have been inferred about women's occupational mobility at different points in their life cycle. Few studies have had access to individuals' work history data, or when they have they have not explored the sequential effects and consequences in individuals' experiences of earlier events. This study sets out to explore these effects.

Studies in Britain touching on occupational mobility have documented the downgrading which women experience at some points in their life cycle. Joshi's (1984) analysis of the WES data found that 18 per cent of women whose highest occupational classification by 1980 was in teaching were currently (or recently) in a lower ranking occupation and the equivalent percentage for women whose highest occupation was nursing or intermediate non-manual work was 39 per cent. Elias

(1983) has documented more of this occupational downgrading from the National Training Survey data as have Stewart and Greenhalgh (1982, 1984).

Occupational downgrading in Britain has also been seen to be linked to discontinuities in women's labour force experience. Stewart and Greenhalgh (1982) found that 25 per cent of women aged 45–54 with an uninterrupted work history were in managerial, professional or technical occupations whereas only 13 per cent of women of this age group were in this occupation when they had two or more breaks from work. Their general conclusions were that job continuity tends to preserve occupational position and breaks in employment are associated with downward occupational mobility. Elias (1983) extended this work on the same data and reached similar conclusions. In all cases, women's breaks from employment are assumed to be because of childbirth.

Studies of occupational mobility in the USA have compared women's and men's occupational attainment. They have often been concerned to explain the failure of women's occupational profiles to reach the same levels of attainment as those of men. Some recent studies have conducted an investigation of occupational attainment in the context of a series of job transitions over time (Tuma, 1976; Felmlee, 1982) or as an explication of the concept of a career Spilerman, 1977; Rosenfeld, 1979, 1980). These studies have found that women fail to make gains in status because of discontinuities in their employment to some extent. The discontinuities are then assumed to be caused by family formation. The studies also show, however, that the differences between men's and women's work histories are only part of the explanation of the status or wage gap between them,[1] and that women receive lower returns to their human capital. Women have been found to have fewer opportunities for gains in occupational status over their lifetime, and women's occupational attainment seems to depend more on formal qualifications than on previous achievements in the labour force. A study of job changing within and between firms by Felmlee (1982) found that job changing within a firm was better for women's prospects and occupational attainment than job changing between firms. Here again women can be assumed to be at a disadvantage if they have discontinuities in their working experiences which mean that they have more between-firm job changing. Shaw (1983) demonstrated that American women's occupational segregation over childbirth did not change very significantly, but that women who did have children had less chance of entering the non-traditional jobs opening up which continuous workers were able to enter. One study in the USA has specifically attempted to examine the effects of motherhood using the number of childbirths (Sorensen, 1983) and has found that children may primarily affect the timing of their mother's career but not her gains in status once she has decided to return to the labour force.

These studies point to a set of relationships which British and American women share; that downward occupational mobility does occur because of breaks from work at childbirth. This study will confirm this finding by examining individual transitions across the break for childbirth. It is also possible to quantify the extent to which women have such experiences, and to see whether childbirth is the main time when downward mobility is experienced by British women. In the main the analysis focuses on individuals' lifetime experiences although an aggregate analysis of occupational transitions between the 12 occupational categories is provided in Appendix 2.

VERTICAL OCCUPATIONAL MOBILITY

Any examination of vertical occupational mobility up or down an occupational scale can only be carried out if a vertical occupational move can be identified. This is not as straightforward as it might at first appear. We have a list of occupational categories in Table 3.1 and, broadly speaking, those at the top end clearly have a higher status and income than those at the bottom end. The problems start to arise if we want to make precise judgements about occupations which are, say, all at the bottom end, or, all in the middle range. As we noted in Chapter 2, at least some of the disputes about women's place in class analysis have involved the issue of where women's sales work should appear in a ranking of occupations.

This identification problem was resolved here in a number of complementary ways. In the first case, the identification of a set of profiles of movements, the disruptions to these profiles, and women's preferences to get back to their original profile subsequently, help to identify some of the norms of women's occupational mobility. An identification of the norm means that deviations from it can also be described. So, for example, a woman who followed a clerical profile up to experiencing the disruption of having to move because of her husband's job, who then took a shop assistant job, but soon returned to clerical work and continued in it, could be identified as having experienced downward occupational mobility. These types of experiences happened sufficiently frequently to map out the vertical moves. As we saw in the previous chapter, movements between the semi-skilled jobs at the bottom of the WES list of occupations were described as a profile, or a norm; in this sense these movements were not thought to constitute vertical moves.

Small-scale qualitative studies have also described the profiles identified here without any mention of women experiencing their job moves as vertically mobile; this is further support for the ranking which emerges from the profiles of experiences. Lastly, identification of vertical mobility comes from a ranking of occupations by earnings which Joshi (1984) undertook. The ranking which emerged consistently from all of these sources is set out below, starting at the highest:

1. Professional/teacher
2. Nursing
3. Intermediate non-manual
4. Clerical
5. Skilled
6. Semi-skilled factory
7. All other occupations (i.e. sales, child care, semi-skilled domestic, other semi-skilled and probably unskilled).

Professional occupations are grouped together with teachers in this list because there were so few professionals in the WES sample. It may well be the case, if a more extensive sample were available, that professionals would be seen to be of a higher rank than teachers. Similarly, at the other end of the scale, some unskilled jobs may be of a lower rank than other semi-skilled work; again it was difficult to distinguish between unskilled and semi-skilled jobs in this survey.

The most significant problem with this set of definitions and the measures which rest on them is the fact that not all movements between clerical work and other semi-skilled occupations are vertical occupational movements. The figures below, indicating the amounts of vertical mobility, are thought therefore to be over-estimates of the amounts of vertical occupational mobility. In addition, women were asked, as part of their work history, about movements between supervisor and ordinary employee status. These movements have been included below in the amounts of vertical mobility, but there is a problem here also. Downward movements out of supervisor status in many cases were accompanied by occupational changes, thus the downward occupational moves only register the one occupational

Table 4.1   Most common downwardly mobile destination occupations

Profile	Downwardly mobile destination occupation
Teacher	Clerical, semi-skilled (not shop assistant)
Nurse	Clerical, semi-skilled
Clerical	Shop assistant, semi-skilled domestic
Semi-skilled factory	Semi-skilled domestic, shop assistant, unskilled
Semi-skilled	(possibly unskilled)

change whereas in fact two changes of occupational status have occurred. Upward mobility into supervisor status, however, which constitutes approximately one fifth of all upward vertical occupational mobility was rarely associated with an occupational change and was more likely to be in the same occupation; presumably this feature is identifying internal labour markets for women, albeit in a limited way. These features of the statistics reported below should therefore be noted.

Downward (or upward) vertical occupational mobility for the purposes of this analysis is defined as a movement either down (or up) on the above scale, or as a movement between supervisor and non-supervisory status. Whilst any upward or downward movement on this scale was possible, in practice some routes were commonly experienced both down and subsequently back up the scale. These common routes are set out in Table 4.1. What is missing from this definition of vertical mobility is any within-category movements of a vertical kind which this survey has not been able to identify. Nonetheless the calculation of the amount of vertical occupational mobility experienced between these occupational categories is an important step in assessing the extent of this experience for women.

DOWNWARD OCCUPATIONAL MOBILITY

The amounts of downward occupational mobility are listed in Table 4.2 for women of different ages and for women with or without children. The figures display the proportions of women in each age group who had at some stage in their employment history experienced either one or more downward moves. Not surprisingly the percentage of women who have ever experienced downward occupational

Table 4.2   Amount of downward occupational mobility

Number of downward occupational transitions	16–19	20–29	30–39	40–49	50–59
Age group, per cent					
At least *ONE*	12	37	52	57	61
At least *TWO*	—	10	15	20	22
At least *THREE*	—	2	3	5	7
N = number in age group who have worked	303	1232	1410	1135	1157
Women with children, per cent					
At least *ONE*	13	44	53	59	63
N = women with children who have worked	(30)	(650)	(1235)	(1003)	(1004)
Childless women, per cent					
At least *ONE*	12	32	47	45	49
N = women without children who have worked	(273)	(582)	(175)	(132)	(153)

mobility increased as their age increased; obviously, the longer is one's employment record, the more chance there is of experiencing occupational mobility of any kind. In the over 50s group, 61 per cent of the women had had at least one experience of downward mobility whereas only 37 per cent of women aged 20 to 29 had had this experience. Experiencing two or more moves down the occupational scale over a lifetime was rare and only 7 per cent of the 50 to 59 age group had at least three experiences of downward mobility.

Women with children have had more experiences of downward mobility than childless women; 59 per cent of women aged 40–49 with children, but only 45 per cent of childless women had had at least one downward move; and the gap is maintained irrespective of age. We would have expected this finding on the basis of other studies. What is perhaps more surprising is that the gap is not wider. We might have expected childless women to have far less experience of downward mobility. The fact that half of them have had this experience by the end of their working life suggests that there are some important causes, other than childbirth. In the case of the 50–59 year age group, being demobbed after the war could have produced this experience.[2] The fact that 45 per cent of childless women aged 40–49 also had at least one experience of downward occupational mobility suggests that the large frequencies cannot be attributable to special circumstances like the war. Childless women appear to have their experience of downward mobility mainly between the ages of 20 and 40 since; after that age, the figures hardly increase. The question of what causes this mobility, if it is not childbirth, will be examined below.

UPWARD OCCUPATIONAL MOBILITY

The amounts of upward occupational mobility are displayed in Table 4.3. There is an increase in the frequency with age and experiencing two or more upwardly mobile moves is far less likely than experiencing one such move. By the end of their working lives, however, 63 per cent of these women had had at least one upwardly mobile move. Childless women had more occurrences of upward moves than women with children, especially between the ages of 30 and 39.

One of the most interesting features of the quantities of upward occupational mobility listed in Table 4.3 is their similarity in size to the frequencies of downward occupational mobility. For each age group there appear to be similar amounts of downward and upward occupational mobility. However, approximately one-fifth of upward mobility consists of movements into supervisor status whereas far fewer of the downward occupational movements are solely movements out of supervisor status. The marked increase with age of an upward mobility experience again disappears when the 54 women are excluded whose experience resulted from their working during the war. These figures do not reveal whether the women who experienced downward occupational mobility were the same ones to experience upward occupational mobility.

UPWARD AND DOWNWARD OCCUPATIONAL
MOBILITY

The way in which women combined experiences of vertical occupa-

Table 4.3   Amount of upward occupational mobility

Number of upward occupational transitions	16–19	20–29	30–39	40–49	50–59
Age Groups, per cent					
At least *ONE*	17	40	51	57	63
At least *TWO*	1	12	18	22	28
At least *THREE*	—	3	5	8	9
N = number in age group who have worked	303	1232	1410	1135	1157
Women with children, per cent					
At least *ONE*	7	39	49	56	63
N = women with children who have worked	(30)	(650)	(1235)	(1003)	(1004)
Childless women, per cent					
At least *ONE*	18	42	67	61	67
N = women without children who have worked	(273)	(582)	(175)	(132)	(153)

tional mobility is displayed in Table 4.4. The figures illustrate that the majority of women had both at least one experience of downward and one experience of upward mobility; 45 per cent of women aged 40–49 with children had this combination, 50 per cent of the 50–59 year group, and 37 per cent of childless women aged 40–49 also had the same set of experiences. The likelihood of experiencing both of these events again increases with age, not surprisingly; only 26 per cent of women with children and 22 per cent of childless women, both aged 20–29 had had both an upward and a downward move. The percentages of those without any experience of vertical mobility decreased with age. The same age effect is not apparent in the percentages of women with only one experience of vertical mobility, either up or down, especially for women with children. These types of experience are minority ones only; 12 per cent of women with children aged 50–59 had had downward (but not upward) occupational

Table 4.4 Experiences of combinations of upward and downward vertical mobility over lifetime

Experiences of vertical occupational mobility*	Women with children					Childless women				
	16–19	20–29	30–39	40–49	50–59	16–19	20–29	30–39	40–49	50–59
Age groups, per cent										
Both upward and downward mobility	3	26	37	45	50	6	22	35	37	41
Downward but no upward	9	17	15	13	12	6	9	7	4	2
Upward but no downward	3	11	12	10	12	12	19	25	19	18
No vertical mobility	84	46	36	31	27	76	50	32	40	39
Total	100	100	100	100	100	100	100	100	100	100
N =	32	676	1254	1016	1025	276	608	194	145	175

*Reference in each case is to at least one experience of particular type.

mobility and 12 per cent had had upward (but not downward) mobility over their working life.

In the childless group, a higher percentage than was the case for women with children were without any experience of vertical mobility, as we have already seen. Perhaps more significantly, childless women did have more experience of upward mobility (without any downward mobility). In the 50–59 year age group, 18 per cent of childless women had at least one upward occupational move but no downward movement (compared with 12 per cent of women with children) and only 2 per cent of the childless had downward but no upward movements (12 per cent for women with children).

This examination of both types of vertical mobility illustrate that the upward (or downward) occupational mobility figures on their own would not represent women's experience on the occupational hierarchy. What seems most likely is that downward movements are followed by upward moves which are a retrieval of an earlier status which is lost during their work cycle. This pattern was part of the description of profiles and their disruptions in the last chapter. The figures illustrate that having children decreases a woman's chance of upward occupational mobility and increases the chance of downward occupational mobility, but there are sufficiently large proportions of women with children experiencing upward occupational mobility and childless women experiencing downward occupational mobility to indicate, again, that differences in women's experiences of childbirth are by no means the whole explanation of different experiences of vertical occupational mobility.

TIMING OF VERTICAL MOBILITY

We have already seen something of the way experiences of vertical occupational mobility occur at different ages. Both downward and upward mobility showed marked increases in frequency when women were between the ages of 20 and 40. The fact that women with children had more experiences of downward mobility than childless women gave the impression that childbirth and childrearing are causes of downward occupational mobility but this may not be the case. We can be more precise about the timing of women's experiences of vertical mobility since the complete work history records of these women were available. An examination of the timing of downward mobility will help to locate the origin of the experience more precisely.

The timing of vertical mobility experiences over the life cycle of women with children is displayed in Table 4.5. Women's life cycle experiences are split into four stages; up to their first birth, their last job before their first birth to the first job after childbirth, any returns to work between childbirths after the first, and job changes since the return after their last child. These figures are the percentages of all experiences of vertical occupational mobility, including supervisor changes, which occurred during the various work cycle phases. The base on which these percentages are calculated, therefore, is *not* the number of women with such an experience, but the number of vertical occupational movements for this group of women – and some women, as we have seen, have more than one.

The age groups over 30 have a fairly stable pattern of downward occupational mobility experiences. Approximately one third of the moves took place during the initial work phase before childbirth and another quarter over the first break for childbirth. In the case of women who are old enough to have finished their childrearing phase (40–59 years), both have approximately one quarter of their downward occupational mobility experiences in their final work phase – the rest being between births. In the younger age groups, under 30, downward occupational mobility was relatively more frequent before childbirth, presumably because these women have not progressed very far through their work cycle.

The amount of downward occupational mobility occurring over the childrearing phase is by far the greatest; 40–45 per cent of all downward moves occurred at this time for most age groups. The percentage of downward moves which occurred over the transition from the last job before childbirth to the first job after childbirth, is very high at 25 per cent. This is a very high proportion when we remember that this is a single occupational transition. The other phases can cover a large number of job changes and therefore, at least in theory, a higher absolute number of experiences of vertical occupational mobility. Thus the findings provide some support for Chaney's (1981) findings from her small-scale study that much of the downward occupational mobility took place over the first childbirth break. It must be noted however, that childbirth is far from being the only significant time when women experience downward occupational mobility and that over half of these experiences take place outside the childrearing phase.

The pattern which emerges from the upward occupational mobility figures in Table 4.5 is quite different from the timing of the downward movements. There is again some variation with age which is a result of

Table 4.5 Timing of downward and upward occupational mobility for women with children

	Downward mobility					Upward mobility				
	16–19	20–29	30–39	40–49	50–59	16–19	20–29	30–39	40–49	50–59
Age groups at interview, per cent										
Up to first birth	(50)	52	36	33	35	(100)	74	53	41	43
First birth to first return	(25)	17	25	24	22	—	4	6	7	10
Second or later births to return after last child	(25)	23	20	17	15	—	9	14	11	9
Since last child	—	8	19	26	28	—	13	27	41	38
Total	100	100	100	100	100	100	100	100	100	100
N* =	4	371	868	860	903	3	334	869	871	1006

*Sample consists of total number of vertical occupational changes.

the different stage of completion of the work cycle. Upward occupational mobility most frequently occurs during the initial work phase or during the final work phase for women who have children. Approximately 80 per cent of upward occupational mobility movements take place during these two phases, with slightly higher proportions during the initial work phase. It is still the case that upward mobility during the initial work phase can be a retrieval of status lost by a disruption, for example, by moving at marriage, rather than being an indicator of occupational advancement – although some of the latter does occur. Some of the upward moves prior to childbirth are promotions to supervisor status. Upward occupational mobility occurs least frequently over the first break for childbirth; only 6–10 per cent of all cases. It is perhaps worth noting, however, that there is some upward occupational mobility over family formation.

These two sets of figures provide a consistent picture; a large amount of downward occupational mobility occurs over the childbirth phase and only a small amount of upward occupational mobility. Much of the downward and upward occupational mobility cancels out for these women rather than showing a net decline or improvement in status. Very few of the jobs held before childbirth were part-time jobs so that downward occupational mobility during this phase, which is approximately one third of all downward movements cannot be linked to women's part-time working status. On the other hand, the higher proportion of upward mobility which occurs during the initial work phase may be linked to the predominance of full-time jobs at this time.

JOB LEAVING REASONS

The reasons women gave for leaving their jobs before an experience of vertical occupational mobility, are listed in aggregate in Table 4.6 for all vertical movements. These reasons provide insights into some of the origins of vertical mobility. Vertical occupational moves occurred for a wide range of reasons, although some are far more frequent than others. The reasons associated with childrearing account for 33 per cent of downward occupational moves which is a large proportion of these transitions.[3] It was a far smaller proportion, 10 per cent, in the case of upward occupational moves, although it is perhaps surprising that this figure is so high. A further high proportion of downward occupational moves (28 per cent), followed the voluntary leaving of jobs because of dissatisfaction. (It is difficult to believe that movement

Table 4.6   Main reason for leaving job preceding vertical occupational
            mobility (%)

Main reason for leaving job	Prior to downward occupational mobility	Prior to upward occupational mobility
Temporary	3	6
Involuntary job separation	7	5
Dissatisfaction/or better job found	28	40
Illness	4	3
Go to college	1	4
Pregnant	19	7
Marriage	6	3
Look-after-home	8	1
Look-after-sick/elderly	1	1
Move-because-of husband's job	4	3
Move-for-other reason	5	4
Other	10	2
Employer changes*	3	20†
Total	100	100
N (of job changes)	4061‡	3851§

*Excluding maternity leave.
†The vast majority of upward mobility here occurs for reason 24 'Changed
Job' and these constitute most of the changes to Supervisor status.
‡Excludes 71 demob reasons for over 50 age group
§Excludes 54 demob reasons for over 50 age group

to a better job was the reason when downward occupational mobility
followed, although this cannot be ruled out.) This is perhaps also
surprising and worth noting. Reasons traditionally thought to apply to
women, like looking after sick or elderly relatives are a very low
proportion (1 per cent). These may of course represent a higher
proportion of all job leaving reasons but these are not so often direct
causes of these women's downward occupational mobility.

Upward occupational mobility appeared to take place for two main
reasons: women found better jobs (40 per cent of moves) or they
became supervisors in their existing jobs (approximately 20 per cent).
Whilst it is not a large figure, 4 per cent of upward occupational

transitions succeed a period of full-time education – which was the experience of only a very small minority of these women. In addition, it is worth noting that whilst involuntary sorts of job leaving reasons (e.g. temporary jobs, dismissals, redundancies, moving because of husband's job, looking after sick etc.) were the events preceding downward occupational mobility, they could also precede upward occupational transitions in a small number of cases. We must beware of thinking therefore that women's experiences are wholly determined, to their disadvantage, by such experiences.[4]

These figures illustrate that the same events can precede either downward or upward occupational mobility and can occur at times throughout women's work cycles. There are some important variations however which are more likely to link certain events to a certain type of vertical occupational mobility – and to a certain time in women's work cycle experiences; childbirth, marriage and domestic reasons are an obvious case in point. This general and more aggregate level of discussion has illustrated that vertical occupational mobility, according to the occupational classification used in this survey, is a widespread experience. It occurs over all phases of women's work cycles as well as over the periods of labour market withdrawals for childbirth and childrearing – but undoubtedly childbirth is a large and important time when downward occupational mobility takes place. However, it is not necessarily a permanent lowering of occupational status. We can now go on to examine, in detail, experiences of vertical occupational mobility over the family formation period to see how they relate to the earlier and subsequent occupational profiles.

VERTICAL MOBILITY OVER FAMILY FORMATION

Much of women's downward occupational mobility occurs, as we have seen, across their first break from work for childbirth. The occupational transitions between the last job before childbirth and the first job after childbirth are displayed in Table 4.7 for all women who had ever returned to work after having at least one child. The diagonal elements reveal the proportions of those who set out in a certain occupation who retained their occupational status at their first return to work. The sizes of the diagonal elements show that teachers are most likely to retain their status (as are professionals but they are a very small group); at this time 85 per cent of women who were teachers before childbirth were still in teaching at their first return to work after

First job after child-birth

Last job before childbirth	Professional	Teacher	Nurse	Intermediate non-manual	Clerical	Sales	Skilled	Child care	Semi-skilled factory	Semi-skilled domestic	Other semi-skilled	Un-skilled	Total	N =
Professional	91	—	—	—	9	—	—	—	—	—	—	—	100	71
Teacher	—	85	2	2	1	3	4	1	1	1	1	—	100	115
Nurse	—	3	61	1	6	7	4	3	1	10	3	2	100	160
Intermediate non-manual	—	3	3	39	19	19	—	2	2	5	3	5	100	62
Clerical	1	—	2	2	49	14	3	4	6	11	3	6	100	964
Sales	—	—	4	2	8	37	3	4	11	14	6	10	100	376
Skilled	—	—	4	3	6	10	43	3	12	7	2	11	100	240
Childcare	—	—	—	—	—	19	6	13	25	19	6	13	100	16
Semi-skilled factory	—	—	1	—	3	10	3	2	52	12	4	14	100	754
Semi-skilled domestic	—	—	2	—	3	8	6	—	17	43	5	16	100	126
Other semi-skilled	—	—	—	—	1	6	4	3	12	14	39	19	100	142
Unskilled	—	—	—	2	5	—	—	—	12	24	7	50	100	42
Proportion of each first return occupation which is part-time job	82	56	71	54	63	72	60	86	53	83	64	94		N = 3008

*Sample: All women with children who have ever returned to work after childbirth, excluding any occupations inadequately described.

childbirth. Over one half of nurses and semi-skilled factory workers also retained their status. Intermediate non-manual, sales, childcare, and other semi-skilled workers have the least chance of being in the same occupation after childbirth; these occupations experienced large outflows. At most, 39 per cent of women who were in these semi-skilled occupations before childbirth were still in them afterwards.

Most of the movement out of occupations at the top of the list is downward vertical mobility. There is a small amount of upward mobility. Much of the movement at the bottom of the list of occupations is horizontal mobility between the various types of semi-skilled work. The occupations which received large inflows at women's first return after childbirth were sales, semi-skilled domestic, unskilled and semi-skilled factory work. The vast majority of the jobs in the first three of these occupations are part-time, as the bottom row of the table illustrates. These results suggest that there is a relationship between the experience of downward occupational mobility and the move to part-time work, but this needs to be tested in the context of a multivariate model. Such a model is described later in this chapter.

A further analysis of the occupational transitions across this first break from employment for childbirth found that women who returned to work after their first child tended to experience less downward occupational mobility than women whose first return came after several children, Dex (1984). This relationship also needs to be tested in a multivariate model when the effects of spending longer out of work are controlled for. Women who returned to work after one child will include, of course, the group of women who took maternity leave and who consequently protected their occupational status over this first break from paid work for childbirth. Even when those taking maternity leave were excluded from the sample, women who returned after one child experienced less downward occupational mobility than those returning for the first time after more than one child.

MODEL OF DOWNWARD OCCUPATIONAL MOBILITY

A multivariate model was constructed of the determinants of women's experiences of downward occupational mobility across the first break from work for childbirth. A dependent dichotomous variable was constructed according to whether a woman had experienced downward occupational mobility. The multivariate analysis tested and quantified the significance of a set of potential influences on women's experiences at this time. The analysis was carried out on the sample of women who had had at least one child, who had returned to work at least once since childbirth, and who could have experienced downward occupational mobility. Women at the bottom of the occupational ranking before childbirth were excluded from the sample on the grounds that they could not have experienced downward occupational mobility; that is, women with a semi-skilled profile before childbirth were excluded. The sample is biased in a number of ways, therefore, and the sizes of the relationships found to exist between certain variables should not be treated as definitive.[5]

The model tests whether a woman's occupational mobility across childbirth was related to her last job before childbirth (OCC1 to OCC5),[6] her duration of time out of the labour market (TIME), whether she returned to a full or part-time job (PART), her educational qualifications (QUAL1, QUAL2),[7] her age (COHORT), her attitudes (ATT) and her duration of working experience before childbirth (WORK).

A full set of the variables included with their precise definitions are set out in Table 4.8.

Given that the variable we are seeking to explain – downward occupational mobility – is dichotomous, taking the value of zero or one, the appropriate estimation technique is a logit regression analysis.[8] Instead, the ordinary least squares (OLS) results are cited here, partly because they are easier to interpret, and the logit coefficients did not differ very significantly from those obtained using OLS (Perry, 1986). A list of the regression results for the WES women is displayed in Table 4.9.

The likelihood of experiencing downward occupational mobility clearly increased if the first return job is part time. The amount of the increase is as much as 29 per cent. Taking a part-time job on returning to work after childbirth therefore has serious consequences. Every additional year spent out of work before the first return also increases the likelihood of experiencing downward occupational mobility on one's return but by a very small amount.

Women's previous occupations had some sizeable effects on women's occupational mobility at this time. Having been a teacher or a nurse reduced the chances of downward mobility by as much as 25 per cent for teachers; the figure for nurses was not significant. Women in intermediate non-manual, clerical or skilled jobs before childbirth had an increased likelihood of downward mobility; by 16 per cent, 8 per

Table 4.8   List of variables in regression on downward occupational mobility

DOWN	dichotomous dependent variable = 1 if woman experienced downward occupational mobility between last job before childbirth and first job after.
PART	If job of first return after childbirth is part time, variable = 1, zero if full time.
TIME	Time spent not working between date of birth of first child and first return to work, to nearest year.
OCC1	Occupational dummy variable = 1 if last job before first birth was either Professional or Teacher.
OCC2	Occupational dummy variable = 1 if last job before first birth was nurse.
OCC3	Occupational dummy variable = 1 if last job before first birth was intermediate non-manual.
OCC4	Occupational dummy variable = 1 if last job before first birth was clerical.
OCC5	Occupational dummy variable = 1 if last job before first birth was skilled.
QUAL1	Qualifications dummy variable = 1 if woman left school with CSEs (not grade 1), clerical or trade apprentice qualifications.
QUAL2	Qualification dummy variable = 1 if woman left school with O levels, CSE grade 1, or City and Guilds.
COHORT	Birth cohorts 5 year age groups 1 = 1920–1925, 9 = 1960–1965.
ATT	Attitudinal dummy variable = 1 if woman thinks women with preschool children should not work (recorded at interview).
WORK	Working experience before childbirth measured to nearest year.

cent and 8 per cent respectively, in comparison with semi-skilled factory jobs. Having some educational qualifications upon leaving school also reduced the chances of downward mobility across childbirth by as much as 12 per cent. As the working experience of women prior to childbirth increased, the likelihood of downward mobility decreased. Women who expressed traditional attitudes were more likely to experience downward mobility. The age of the woman appeared to be unimportant since it was insignificant.

This set of variables together only explain a fairly small amount of the variation in women's experiences of occupational mobility across childbirth, but they are all very significant. We might have expected

Table 4.9 Downward occupational mobility OLS regression results

Variable	Coefficient	t value
PART	0.285	13.8
TIME	0.001	5.7
OCC1	− 0.254	5.8
OCC2	− 0.045	1.1
OCC3	0.162	2.7
OCC4	0.084	3.5
OCC5	0.076	2.2
QUAL1	− 0.126	4.3
QUAL2	− 0.094	3.4
COHORT	− 0.000	0.1
ATT	0.035	1.8
WORK	− 0.007	2.6
R^2	0.14	
N^*	2466	

*Sample: Women with children who have ever returned to work since childbirth and who did not have a semi-skilled profile before childbirth.

that the higher one's occupation to start with the more likely one would be to experience downward occupational mobility, but these results show that there is no necessary relationship of this kind. It is almost the reverse, and the higher one's occupation the greater one's security of keeping it. This analysis is not able to examine any changes in occupational status which may have taken place within an occupational category of course, so that we only have a part of the story here and there may be considerably more experiences of downward occupational mobility than we are capturing. Part-time teachers in Britain, for example, are usually paid at the lowest point on the scale.

The results highlight the importance of women's move into part-time work after childbirth. This move has the biggest single effect on a woman's chances of downward mobility at this time, although her previous occupation is also important. The other significant effects were much smaller. The results suggest that downward mobility is partly a result of choices women make; in particular their preference for part-time work after childbirth. Such choices need to be viewed in the context of constraints women face. Part-time work is often the only way women can combine paid employment and the responsibilities for child care in Britain. Comparisons with the USA reveal that women and households can choose different combinations of paid working hours and child care arrangements when social policies and possibly earnings change (Dex and Shaw, 1986). The consequences for women's careers, of taking a part-time job after childbirth are considerable, but this is largely because the bulk of part-time jobs are the lower level occupations. Women are often faced with the choice, therefore, of working full time to keep their occupational status, or accepting a loss of status in order to get a part-time job. Policy implications emerge from this dilemma which are discussed in the final chapter.

MOBILITY OVER A LIFETIME

In earlier sections women's occupational experiences before and over childbirth have been examined. We can also document occupational mobility in later life and indeed over the whole lifetime of the older women in this survey. This section relies on information from those aged 40 to 59 recognising that the youngest women in this group still have a lengthy potential working life ahead of them. Table 4.10 summarises their mobility experiences up until their most recent job.

Women with teaching profiles are clearly the most likely to retain their status throughout their working life; 70 per cent remained in teaching throughout. After teaching, clerical work is the next most secure occupation in that 50 per cent managed to stay in some form of clerical work. Nurses have a much lower likelihood of staying in nursing across their family formation break from work and this is approximately the same extent as skilled and semi-skilled factory workers, although part of this mobility in nursing may be caused by the broad nature of the nursing occupational category.

Downward occupational mobility was highest out of nursing, skilled and clerical work. There are clearly fewer opportunities for downward mobility when one is near the bottom of the occupational hierarchy; nonetheless it is not the case that the higher the occupational profile the greater the downward mobility, as we noted earlier. Teachers had very low proportions of downward mobility experiences. Teachers who did lose their status however were least likely to recover it

Table 4.10   Occupational profile experiences of 40–59 age groups*

Profile before childbirth	After starting in profile before childbirth			
	per cent remaining in it throughout	per cent experiencing downward mobility at first return after childbirth	per cent recovering status after losing it over childbirth	per cent most recent job in same occupation as profile before childbirth
Teacher	70	19	0	79
Nurse	30	43	19	59
Clerical	50	37	32	62
Skilled	29	42	32	30
Semi-skilled factory	26	15	95	41
Semi-skilled	†	(11)	28	71

* Sample based on women with at least one childbirth who ever returned to work, aged 40–59 in 1980.
†Difficult to determine.

subsequently. Nurses also had seemingly few opportunities to regain their status. Semi-skilled factory workers by contrast had approximately a 95 per cent chance of regaining their occupational status having lost it, and the other profiles all had around one third who recovered their status.

The percentages of those whose most recent job was in the same occupation as their occupational profile before childbirth are quite high in some cases. Certainly more women had a most recent job in their initial profile than stayed in the profile throughout, not surprisingly. Groups who tended to retain their status throughout, like teachers and clerical workers, also had high proportions whose most recent job was in teaching; 79 per cent of women who had a teaching profile before childbirth had a most recent job in teaching and 62 per cent of the early clerical workers were most recently employed in clerical work. Nurses tended to lose their status at some point over their lifetime, but the fact that 59 per cent of those starting out in nursing were in this occupation in their most recent job suggests that it is easier to return to this occupation than it is to return to, say, skilled work.

The amount of vertical mobility experienced over a lifetime clearly varies enormously between occupations. Teachers, as we have seen, have the least mobility in this respect. The results have also shown that the considerable loss of occupational status women experienced over childbirth was not a permanent loss for a sizeable group of women, although the majority did seem to lose their status permanently; at least, up until their interview in 1980. Since some of these women are only in their early forties, the recovery rates are probably underestimates of what might ultimately occur. The move into part-time work had serious consequences for women's occupational status. The move back to full-time work that some women make after childrearing helps them to recover lost status (Dex, 1984). Of course, by having breaks from work, women still suffer losses of seniority and promotion within jobs; for example, in teaching, where disrupted service can often mean that one keeps restarting at the bottom of the scale. The costs to women's careers of having children are high therefore, as Joshi (1985) points out.[9]

CONCLUSIONS

An examination of women's occupational histories has shown that vertical mobility occurs throughout all of their life-cycle stages. Whilst childbirth is undoubtedly the biggest single cause of vertical downward occupational mobility, many childless women also lose their occupational status at some point over their working lives. To some extent, the loss of occupational status is balanced by upward mobility, and in these cases the downward move is not permanent. For a significant number, the downward move is permanent. When it occurs over childbirth, it is more likely to be caused by a move to part-time work, because part-time work in Britain is predominantly the lower paid jobs at the bottom end of the occupational hierarchy. Women's choice of part-time work needs to be seen in the context of the division of labour within the home where they usually have the primary responsibility for child care. It is however the structure of opportunities, whereby part-time jobs are 'crummy' jobs, which makes the choice of a part-time job so detrimental to women's careers, and wasteful.

This examination of women's occupational mobility over their lifetime has some relevance to the conclusions which can be drawn from cross-sectional occupational distributions. At the end of the previous chapter it was concluded that one could infer something about women's lifetime employment status from the cross-sectional occupations. We need to add a caveat to that conclusion which arises from the findings on vertical occupational mobility described in this chapter. Cross-sectional studies will not reflect the occupations in which many women spend most of their time, when they occur immediately after a period of not working for childbirth, or when they are employed in part-time jobs, or when the previous job ended involuntarily (dismissal, redundancy, illness, move because of husband's job). The first two of these reasons are effectively the same reason. Asking women what was their last job before childbirth would serve to identify the extent of any misinterpretation. Given that adjustments of this kind could be made it would be possible to estimate the frequencies of women's lifetime occupational profiles from cross-sectional data.

These records of women's experiences of occupational mobility over their lifetime also provide some data upon which better models of the operation of labour markets can be constructed. The model which best fits these data is elaborated more fully in Chapter 6. Suffice it to say here, that the women's labour market is not a single segment of a dual or triple labour market model; there are important sectors within what are essentially 'women's jobs'. In some cases there is mobility between occupations (e.g. semi-skilled) and in some cases not (e.g. teaching). The model clearly needs to incorporate a part-time sector which has both inflows and outflows. The model is also likely to have an industrial as well as an occupational description. In the next chapter women's industrial profiles are examined as a basis for understanding more about women's roles in the labour market structure.

5 Industrial Profiles and Industrial Mobility

INTRODUCTION

Industries form the backbone structure of an economy and determine, to a large extent, the range of occupations on offer. There has been surprisingly little discussion of the role women's employment has played and is playing in the industrial structure, in comparison with much more extensive consideration of women's occupations. The changes in women's employment which have occurred since the Second World War have been clearly linked to industrial changes in Britain. Women's employment has increased in the growing services sector and many of their jobs have been part time. If we are interested in the relationships between the structure of opportunities in the economy and women's employment experiences, we should not omit a consideration of the industrial categories of women's work.

The industrial structure of employment has been changing gradually in Britain for a century or more. If we compare the distribution of jobs by industry over large periods of time, the changes are enormous. The trend is also unmistakable over a short period. Over a twenty-year period, 1940 to 1960, UK manufacturing employment has declined from approximately 39 to 35 per cent and services (including government) increased from approximately 38 to 45 per cent. In the USA over a similar period, manufacturing employment declined from approximately 30 to 25 per cent and services (including government) grew from 41 to 58 per cent. In the 1980s the proportion of employment in services is approaching 70 per cent. It is important to note, however, as Thatcher (1978) points out for the UK, these figures do not necessarily mean that manufacturing employment has declined in absolute terms. In Britain the numbers employed in manufacturing were rising until 1966, since when they have started to fall.

Women's employment has played a large part in these changes. We saw in Chapter 2 that women are now concentrated in certain industries in Britain. Between 1841 and 1971 women increased their share of employment in nearly every industry with the exception of textiles and miscellaneous services. These two cases of decline between 1841 and 1971 result from the decline of the textile industry

90

and the demise of domestic service as an occupation. Since 1961 women's proportion of miscellaneous services' employment has begun to rise again. The growth in women's employment since the Second World War has affected all industries, but services and distribution have seen by far the greatest changes. In Britain over the period from 1966 to 1976 there was a net decline in the employment of manufacturing industries (plus primary industries); of this net decline, 73 per cent were men and 27 per cent were women. Over the same period the net increase in private sector services resulted from a 125 per cent increase for women and a 44 per cent decrease in men's services employment. Of the total growth of the public sector for the same period, three out of every four of the extra jobs went to women (Joseph, 1983).

Much of the increase in women's services and public sector employment has been in part-time work but this aspect of women's work has been given relatively little recognition in the analyses of socio-economic change. In 1976, 40 per cent of workers in the whole economy were working in part-time jobs; between 1971 and 1981 approximately 60 per cent of the employment increases in both miscellaneous services and distribution over the decade were in women's part-time jobs (Dex and Perry, 1984). These figures amount to very large structural changes in the nature of British employment. In Britain, economists have regarded these changes as having grave significance for the health of the British economy. The aspect of these changes which poses a problem largely arises because the open nature of the British economy means that a decline in manufacturing tends to create a balance of payments deficit in Britain (oil revenues are currently protecting Britain from a deficit).

The explanations offered of these sectoral changes have tended to neglect any consideration of the role of women's employment in these changes (Dex, 1985). Discussions have at best merely noted in passing that women's increasing participation has been in the services growth sector. In Britain, the recognition of women's role came as part of a criticism of one of the earliest discussions of the problem. When the gender-based nature of the employment changes were noted it was clear that certain theories could not be correct (Thatcher, 1978); for example, part of Bacon and Eltis's (1976) discussion of Britain's problems suggested that private sector employment (in manufacturing) was being crowded out by the growth of public sector employment. When the employment figures are disaggregated by sex as in Thatcher (1978), it became clear that the growth in public sector jobs in Britain was a growth in women's employment whereas the decline in manufacturing was a decline in men's employment. Since men's and women's employment are highly segregated and on the whole men are not prepared to do 'women's work' it is difficult to argue that women's employment increases in the public sector have crowded out men's manufacturing employment in Britain. One of the latest papers examining the distributional implications of deindustrialisation in Britain (Lovatt and Ham, 1984) also fails to consider the gendered division of employment.

The concept of a reserve army of labour and the theory of segmented labour markets have considered women's role in the industrial structure and they both share the view that women are a marginal workforce. In the case of the reserve army idea, these workers are drawn into and displaced from the labour market according to the needs of capital over business cycle fluctuations and changes in the industrial structure. The question of whether women fit the notion of a reserve army has been debated at a theoretical level and as an empirical issue (Dex, 1985). The empirical work has taken place in Britain in the context of the growth of women's part-time employment in the services and the conclusions reached are that women's location in services has protected them from feeling the worst effects of recessions (Dex and Perry, 1984). These findings do not fit in with the theory and suggest therefore that theoretical work has been inadequate.

The discussions of industrial structure changes, as far as aggregate employment effects are concerned, leave much to be desired. In addition, these discussions leave us with little understanding of how individual women are affected by the industrial structure and how this varies over their life-cycle. One British study of the life-cycle variation of women's employment does exist, Sleeper (1975), but it was conducted at an aggregate level and so is particularly inappropriate to the nature of the task it set itself. However, Sleeper recognised the potential value of examining labour mobility over the life-cycle since it can give us structural information about labour markets. The examination of women's work histories undertaken here will provide more detail about the life-cycle variations in women's industrial employment. A set of women's industrial profiles are described below. They are counterparts to the occupational profiles described in Chapter 3 and they were obtained largely by the same method.

INDUSTRIAL CLASSIFICATION

As was the case with occupations, this analysis is largely dependent on the classification of industries, used in the WES survey, of 9 categories. Industries were broadly divided into manufacturing (4 groups), services (3 groups), distribution and agriculture. The full list of categories is outlined in Table 5.1.

The major problem arising from the industrial classification used was the combining into one category of a private sector service activity, insurance, with all public sector jobs in national or local government. This prevented any examination of certain types of inter-industry movements between private and public sector activities neither could the changes in frequencies of either insurance or public sector jobs be examined. Given these limitations the industrial profiles are described below.

INDUSTRIAL PROFILES

Manufacturing profile – is one in which all the jobs are in one of the four manufacturing categories. (It becomes important to note here that if semi-skilled factory work in the distribution industry is included as a manufacturing industry then a considerably larger frequency of manufacturing profiles result). In a minority of the total cases included here, the jobs were all in one of these manufacturing industries; most often in textiles.

Services profile – is one in which all the jobs are in one of the three service sector categories (or public services). Again, if shop assistant work in retail distribution is included as a service sector industry then the total frequency of service sector profiles increases. In total this is a very large category.

Professional and scientific services profile– is one in which all the jobs are in the one category of professional and scientific services.

Mixed manufacturing services profile – is one in which movement occurs between any or all of both the manufacturing and services and primary industry jobs. Jobs in the primary industry were relatively rare so that they are included here since they are most often found in combination with jobs in other industries.

Primary or agricultural profile – is one in which a woman moves between agricultural or primary industry jobs solely. This category has been included for completeness but it represents the experiences of only a very few women (65 in this sample).[1]

Table 5.1   Industry categories

1. *Food, drink and tobacco processing*
   Processing or manufacture of all food, drink and tobacco products; *not* production of raw materials; not retail or wholesale distribution.
2. *Textiles, clothing, footwear, leather goods*
   Manufacture of all textiles (e.g. wool, rope, carpet, synthetic fibres), clothing, footwear, leather goods, fur; *not* retail or wholesale distribution, not upholstery and bedding.
3. *Engineering, metal goods, metal manufacture*
   Mechanical, instrument, electrical, shipbuilding and marine engineering, manufacture of vehicles and all types of metal goods (excluding toys), metal manufacture (from raw materials); *not* civil engineering.
4. *Other manufacturing industries*
   Manufacture and processing of coal and petroleum products (including oil refining), manufacture of chemicals (e.g. paint, soap, fertilizers), plastics, pharmaceuticals, rubber, bricks, pottery, cement, glass (and goods made of these materials), timber, furniture and other wooden goods, upholstery and bedding, paper, printing and publishing, toys, games, sports equipment, musical instruments.
5. *Distributive trades*
   Wholesale and retail distribution of all goods (all shops including sub post offices), pre-packing of food when no processing involved; *not* road haulage and transport, not filling stations, main post offices, cafes, pubs, etc., dry cleaners.
6. *Professional and scientific services*
   Accountancy, schools (including nursery schools), other educational establishments (including school meals service and educational administration), legal services, hospitals and other medical, dental, research and development services, day nurseries and creches, local authority health and social services (e.g. social workers, people working in LA homes and centres for handicapped), religious organisations.
7. *Insurance, public and local government administration*
   Insurance, banking and other financial institutions, estate agents, property companies, advertising, market research, typing, duplicating, copying services, employment agencies (not government), security firms (not transport), management consultants, Civil Service, armed forces, police, fire service, other local government services not included elsewhere; *not* hospitals, schools, building and civil engineering establishments, training services.
8. *Other services*
   Construction and civil engineering, gas, electricity, water, road haulage, transport, postal services and telecommunications, packing and despatch

Table 5.1 *contd.*   Industry categories

---

of goods (without processing or distribution), travel agents, school crossings, hotels, pubs, restaurants, entertainment and sports services, personal services (e.g. hairdressing, private domestic service, childminding, home helps), laundries, dry cleaners, filling stations, shoe repairers, motor repairers, welfare and charitable services, old people's homes, playgroups, museums, art galleries, trade unions, employers' organisations.

9. *Agriculture, forestry, fishing, mining, quarrying*
   Farming, horticulture, mining and quarrying of coal, stone, slate, extraction of chalk, sand, gravel, gas oil.

FREQUENCIES OF PROFILES

The frequencies of these different types of industrial profiles are set out in Table 5.2 by age. The figures are based on the complete set of jobs held by these women up to the interview in 1980. The mixed manufacturing–services profile is the largest single category characterising 53 per cent of the whole WES sample of women. The services profile is second largest in size covering 30 per cent of the sample. The agricultural profile as indicated is an extremely small and almost nonexistent category; the manufacturing profile has 10 per cent, and the professional and scientific services 7 per cent of the total.

The different age groups have very different experiences. As a general rule the single industry groups (services or manufacturing) find that their proportions decline as age increases and a larger proportion of the older age groups have the mixed manufacturing–services profile. Manufacturing profiles are 20 per cent of the youngest age group but only 9 per cent of the over-fifties group. The professional and scientific services group is a slight exception to this rule in that this group has an increasing proportion up to age 40, but at ages above 40 the percentage declines. The fact that entry to

Table 5.2   Industrial profiles over a woman's whole work history

Industrial profile	Total WES women who have worked at some time (%)	Women by age group at interview Age group (%)				
		16–19	20–29	30–39	40–49	50–59
Manufacturing profile*	9.6	20	12	8	7	9
Services profile†	29.5	53	39	28	24	21
Professional and scientific services profile	7.0	6	8	9	6	4
Mixed manufacturing-services profile‡	53.3	22	41	55	62	66
Agricultural profile	0.5	1	–	–	1	1
Total	100	100	100	100	100	100
N	5236	303	1232	1410	1135	1156

*Includes distribution industry when semi-skilled factory job.
†Includes distribution industry when occupation is not semi-skilled factory.
‡All distribution industry jobs can be included here.

professional occupations have older entry ages than other occupations probably explains the differences. In the youngest age group, the largest category is services representing 53 per cent of the total and both manufacturing and the mixed group having approximately one fifth of this age group. In the oldest group (over 50), 66 per cent have had a mixed manufacturing–services profile, 21 per cent a (wholly) services profile and only 9 per cent a manufacturing profile.

These figures suggest that there is some tendency for women to enter jobs in the services industries after leaving school, a suggestion which we can investigate more fully later from these and other data. Also, to the extent that they enter manufacturing industries, they rarely stay in them over their whole employment career. It is not so surprising that women experience a wider range of industries as they increase in age, but there is more to say about the direction of change and this is pursued as we move now to an alternative approach to the discussion of industrial profiles.

This list of the industrial profile types, of some interest on its own, became more interesting when combined with information on the occupational profiles described earlier. Thus an examination of industrial profiles in the context of occupational profiles was thought to be a more rewarding investigation and one which is pursued more extensively below.

INDUSTRIAL AND OCCUPATIONAL PROFILES

Women do not appear to choose an industry in the same way that they choose an occupation. If individuals are asked what they would like to be, their responses invariably are stated in terms of occupations and not industries. In this sense women's (and men's) careers are determined in part by occupational choices and in part by the availability of industrial opportunities. One might almost think of these two categories as the occupational supply-side choices and the industrial demand-side opportunities of labour markets. Women's choices of occupations, their attachment to them and the disruptions which they experience make certain industrial profiles more or less likely. There are correlations between the type of occupational profiles and the type of industrial profile women experience. These relationships are set out in Table 5.3 and are described below for most of the occupational profiles.

Professionals

Only a very small number of women had a professional occupational profile in this survey and this profile, where it did occur, tended to be movements between jobs in the professional and scientific services industry. The mention of professionals is included here for completeness, but no further discussion is given to this extremely small group.

Semi-professional profiles

There were two major semi-professional occupational profiles, one in teaching, the other in nursing. These two occupational profiles shared

Table 5.3   Industrial profiles to emerge in conjunction with the various occupational profiles of women

Occupational profile	Associated industrial profiles	Likely change with downward occupational mobility
Professional	Professional and Scientific services profile	Services profile or mixed manufacturing–services profile
Semi-professional nurses and teachers	Professional and Scientific services profile	Services profile or mixed manufacturing–services profile
Clerical	Mixed manufacturing–services profile	none
	Services profile	none
	Manufacturing profile	Mixed manufacturing–services profile
Semi-skilled factory	Manufacturing profile	Mixed manufacturing–services profile
Semi-skilled	Mixed manufacturing–services profile	none
	Services profile	none

a common industrial profile in the professional and scientific services industry profile which is the category used in the WES survey to cover both education and the national health service.[2] Intermediate non-manual occupations, the other semi-professional group, could be across a range of industries and therefore across the whole range of industrial profiles but since there were so few of them, they are not discussed any further below.

Entry into teaching does not usually occur before age 21. This is a later age than entry into other profiles and it explains some of the increase with age of this industrial profile experience. Women who entered nursing as their first job did so from age 17 onward. Some became nurses later after starting work in other jobs; in which case they would be more likely to have a services profile, although this depends on the nature of their earlier jobs.

Women did not lose their status as teachers as often as women in other occupations lost their occupational status. Nevertheless disruptive events and breaks from work for childbirth could occur in both teaching and nursing profiles and a change of industrial profile usually followed when a change of occupation occurred. When teachers or nurses lost their status they could end up in skilled or semi-skilled occupations; since these occupations are in manufacturing and service sector industries the change of industrial profile was from professional and scientific services to either a services profile or a mixed manufacturing-services profile.

Clerical profile

The main industrial profiles which are generated by women's attachment to clerical jobs are the mixed manufacturing–services profile, the service sector profile and, to a far lesser extent, the manufacturing profile. By far the largest most frequent profile for clerical workers is the mixed manufacturing–services profile. It is perhaps not so surprising that women who do clerical jobs move between different types of industries since all industries provide some clerical work, although some more than others.

Clerical occupational profiles could also be disrupted either by an event such as an involuntary job separation or over a break from work for childbirth, and there was a significant chance of women experiencing downward occupational mobility as a result. On the whole there was far less change of industrial profiles as a result of changes of occupation – but there are some identifiable paths. A common destination occupation after downward occupational mobility from a clerical profile was into a shop assistant job in the distribution industry. Thus the distribution (services) industry was a frequent employer of the downwardly mobile clerical worker. If the woman's earlier experiences had been a services profile then no overall industrial change was visible from this experience. A distinct change from manufacturing into services was visible when the woman's earlier profile was in manufacturing industries. This meant that at least, in a sizeable proportion of cases, this shift into the service sector could be seen to occur over a break from work for childbirth. It was also commonly a shift into part-time work. The effect on a woman's industrial profile, therefore, of having a break from childbirth, or of experiencing a different disruptive event, could be to change a manufacturing profile into a mixed manufacturing–services profile. Alternatively, there may be no change at all where women already had either a mixed or wholly services profile. Women could recover their occupational status in clerical work subsequently to losing it, but the effects of such an experience on their industrial profiles were difficult to predict.

Upward occupational mobility had little visible effect on women's industrial profiles especially since the most common upward mobility was becoming a supervisor in the same industry.

Semi-skilled factory or skilled

Women who had a skilled or semi-skilled factory profile had only one industrial profile, the manufacturing profile. As they changed jobs between semi-skilled factory or skilled jobs they moved between the four manufacturing industrial categories. In some cases, the jobs were all in the same manufacturing industry, most likely in textiles (which includes clothing). As mentioned earlier, this industrial profile was probably specific to certain regional localities in Britain.

The downward occupational mobility associated with a semi-skilled factory profile was into semi-skilled domestic work, unskilled work or shop assistant work and it occurred, as with other profiles, subsequently to disruptive events or breaks from work for childbirth. A change of industrial profile often resulted because women's new jobs were commonly in the service industries (semi-skilled domestic and shop assistant work). Thus one consequence of downward occupational mobility was a change of industrial profile from manufacturing into a mixed manufacturing–services profile. The transition was often a movement into part-time employment. This sort of experience would lead us to expect to see the frequency of manufacturing profiles declining with increasing age and the figures in Table 5.2 illustrate such a trend. If women retrieved their occupational status in semi-skilled factory work, at a later date, that would still leave them with a mixed manufacturing–services profile. Upward occupational mobility usually occurred through a movement into a supervisor's job in the same industry so that, as previously, upward occupational mobility was not as likely to produce a change of industrial profile.

Semi-skilled

Women who moved between semi-skilled jobs, including (possibly lower grade) clerical jobs, also moved between the whole range of industries and could end up with either a services profile or a mixed manufacturing–services profile. Movements between industries were therefore just as common as the movements between occupational groups which characterised this occupational profile.

Two entry routes into semi-skilled occupational profiles were noted earlier. A large group started out in shop assistant work in the (retail) distribution industry, as noted earlier. This meant that their industrial profile often started out in a service industry, but it could change, both into and later out of manufacturing industries. This starting point in services again coincides with the changes visible in the aggregate figures in Table 5.2. Another entry route into a semi-skilled occupational profile from unskilled work was more likely to be associated with an industrial change from manufacturing into services but this did not involve many women.

Downward occupational mobility was more difficult to distinguish in this occupational profile and the same difficulty carried over into the industrial profiles. Unskilled work was the only discernible downward destination occupation and since that could be in either manufacturing or service industries, no particular change in industrial profile needed to follow.

This set of industrial profiles was produced as women pursued occupational attachments over their working lives, of the sort described in Chapter 3. The mixed manufacturing–services profile, which can be found associated with any of the major occupational profiles illustrates that industrial mobility can be part of a woman's coherent occupational strategy. In this sense, mobility between industries need not be thought to be useless, detrimental or even wasteful, as some have suggested.[3] Similarly movements between the various service industries or different manufacturing industries can also be the result of coherent occupational attachments by these women. Some of the mixed manufacturing–services profiles emerged in association with an experience of downward occupational mobility however. In particular, after a break from work because of childbirth many women returned to part-time work in service or retail distribution industries and a change of industrial profile from a manufacturing to a mixed manufacturing–services profile could result. The same result could occur following on from other disruptive events in women's experiences, for example, moving because of husband's job, or at marriage.

INDUSTRIAL PROFILES OVER A LIFETIME

If we classify women's profiles of industrial movements on the basis of their complete work history (as in Table 5.2) a different picture emerges than if the classification is based solely on their experience up until the first childbirth. The distributions of these two classifications are placed side by side in Table 5.4, for the sample of women with children. Over the whole of their working lives, relatively few women have a manufacturing profile; the percentages are all under 10 per cent for women over 30 years. Up to the birth of their first child, however, the stable figure of approximately 20 per cent of all age groups had a manufacturing profile. The results suggest that women reflect the process of deindustrialisation in their individual experiences, over breaks from work for childbirth. Some start out in manufacturing work, and this experience does not appear to have declined significantly over time, but there is a significant move out of manufacturing over childbirth. We might deduce, therefore, that insofar as manufacturing industries are employers of women, many of them will be young childless women.

There is a steady increase in services profiles both up to the first childbirth and for all of women's working lives, with the youngest group (20–29) having 43 per cent with a services profile prior to childbirth; only 33 per cent of the 50–59 age group had this profile before childbirth. The growth of service industries in the post-war era is therefore reflected here.

We have seen here the picture of women's patterns of industrial movements as a whole. We can now trace the same picture step by step over women's working cycle, starting from their first jobs and moving on to their most recent jobs in 1980.

FIRST JOBS

The figures in Table 5.5 illustrate the proportions of women of the WES sample whose first jobs were in certain industries. There is a remarkable amount of stability in these proportions across all of the ten 5-year age groups. This stability is even more pronounced when the industrial categories are grouped further (see Appendix Table A4.1). Approximately one quarter of all these cohorts of women had a first job in the distribution industry. A further third had first jobs in one of the manufacturing industries, textiles having a higher propor-

Table 5.4 Industrial profile classification on the basis of pre-childbirth experiences in comparison with the whole working experiences of women with children

	Women with children by age at interview (%)							
	20–29		30–39		40–49		50–59	
Industrial profiles	Up to 1st child	All working life	Up to 1st child	All working life	Up to 1st child	All working life	Up to 1st child	All working life
Manufacturing profile	19	14	20	9	22	7	21	8
Services profile and professional and scientific services	43	39	43	36	39	30	33	25
Mixed manufacturing–services profile	37	47	37	55	38	62	44	66
Agricultural profile	1	1	–	–	1	1	2	1
Total	100	100	100	100	100	100	100	100
N		650		1235		1003		1003

Table 5.5 Industry of first jobs (by age at interview)

Industry	Age group (%)								
	16–19	20–24	25–29	30–34	35–39	40–44	45–49	50–54	55+
Food	4	3	3	5	5	7	5	7	5
Textiles etc	11	10	11	11	14	14	16	17	20
Engineering	7	6	9	7	8	7	7	7	8
Other Manufacturing	7	7	8	10	10	9	9	7	8
Distribution	26	26	22	25	24	24	24	22	18
Professional & Scientific services	9	12	18	17	15	13	13	11	7
Insurance local & national government	13	16	14	10	10	8	7	7	7
Miscellaneous services	21	18	14	15	13	15	16	19	24
Agriculture primary	1	1	1	1	2	2	2	4	4
Total	100	100	100	100	100	100	100	100	100
N = *	303	564	668	762	648	584	551	564	593
not available	1	1	–	–	2	2	2	1	3

*Excludes sample who have never worked.

tion than the others, and approximately 40 per cent entered the labour market through one of the service industries; miscellaneous services was the single largest group. Very few had a first job in a primary industry. Some changes over time are visible from an examination of the experiences of different age groups. First the over-55 age group stand out as having some anomalous experiences presumably because of the effects of the Second World War. Certain trends are visible through the other age groups especially in the aggregate industry groupings; a gradual decline occurs in the proportion entering a manufacturing industry and a gradual increase in the proportion entering a service industry; distribution has retained a fairly stable intake on the whole. These trends are not visible to the same extent in all of the separate industries which have been aggregated however. Engineering, as a manufacturing industry has not suffered the same decline in its proportionate entry as the rest of the manufacturing industries. Similarly, professional and scientific services and insurance and government have experienced the steady gradual increase whereas the miscellaneous services category has seen more fluctuations.

These results are interesting since they reflect some of the known changes of industrial structure in Britain over the post-war period. The decline in manufacturing industries and the increase in service industries are well known changes and they are reflected here in this sample of women's first jobs. The implication for women's industrial profiles is that fewer women would be able to have a manufacturing profile as time goes on if fewer women enter these industries and the figures in Table 5.2 illustrated that this was the case for these groups of WES women. Services profiles would be expected to be increasing however. It is also well known that the engineering industry has not been declining steadily over this period, although it has been declining more recently so that the figures for engineering, as portrayed through these women's experiences are as we might expect. The fluctuations of the miscellaneous service industrial category reflect, perhaps, a greater sensitivity to demand fluctuations. These distributions coincide further with what is known about young women's employment; that is, young women are employed predominantly in distribution and miscellaneous services and to a lesser extent in insurance, banking, finance, and professional and scientific services. Thus there is a large measure of overlap between these WES women's experiences and employment structures in Britain in the post-war period.

We can move on to examine the changes of industry exhibited by these women as they move out of their first jobs into others. This analysis will provide more information about women's industrial mobility over the life cycle.

FIRST JOB TO LAST JOB BEFORE CHILDBIRTH

The industrial mobility of women over the period from their first job to their last job before childbirth is displayed, for the aggregate industry categories in Table 5.6. As previously, diagonal cells indicate that

Table 5.6   Industrial mobility between first job and last job before first birth

| First Job | Last job before first birth | | | | | |
	Manufacturing	Distribution	Services	Primary	Total	N
Manufacturing	68	10	21	1	100	1406
Distribution	29	43	27	1	100	900
Services	16	10	71	2	100	1438
Primary	19	10	27	43	100	92

Sample includes women with at least one childbirth who have worked before childbirth – all ages. Excludes any with industry unclassified.

women were in the same industrial category both at the beginning of the period covered and at the end; this is not to say, however, that the woman is in the same job on both occasions. Women who started out in manufacturing or services industries when they left school are those most likely to be in services when they had a break from work for childbirth; 68 and 71 per cent of women starting out in manufacturing or services respectively were in the same broad industrial category later. Only 43 per cent of those starting out in distribution or primary industries were in these categories prior to childbirth; these two industries would therefore appear to have higher turnover. In the case of distribution, this is not surprising, since if it is to remain an employer of young workers there must be a constant shedding of its labour force as they grow older. There may well be both supply and demand considerations in this process as other studies of school leavers' employment and school leavers' preferences for jobs have shown.[4]

Table 5.7   Industrial mobility over childbirth

Last job before first birth	First return job				Sum Row %	N=
	Manufacturing	*Distribution*	*Services*	*Primary*		
Manufacturing	48	14	36	3	100	1188
Distribution	16	40	42	2	100	546
Services	12	13	73	2	100	1202
Primary	11	8	28	53	100	74

Sample includes women with at least one childbirth who worked before childbirth and have returned to work after childbirth at least once – all ages. Excludes any with industry unclassified.

LAST JOB BEFORE TO FIRST JOB AFTER CHILDBIRTH

The industry transitions over the first break for childbirth are displayed in Table 5.7. Here 73 per cent of women in services before childbirth get a job in services on their first return to work. This was the same percentage as stayed in services before childbirth in Table 5.6. Similarly, the proportions staying in distribution and primary industries over childbirth are approximately the same as those seen in the transitions prior to childbirth. There is a notable difference, however, in the sizes of transitions out of manufacturing industries when pre-childbirth experiences are compared with those occurring over childbirth. Prior to childbirth, the percentages of those remaining in manufacturing industries was 68 per cent; 21 per cent moved out of manufacturing into services. Over the break for childbirth, the proportion remaining in manufacturing was only 48 per cent and the proportion who moved from manufacturing into services increased to 36 per cent. There is a similar change in the flow from distribution to services. Before childbirth, 27 per cent of women starting out in distribution made this transition whereas over childbirth the proportion increases to 42 per cent. These two effects together mean that there is a considerable additional shift into services over the childbirth break; this has already been noted in the discussion of individual profiles. There is some movement back from services to manufacturing both over the initial work period before childbirth and over the childbirth break, but it is a trickle in comparison with the shift in the

Table 5.8   Industry of first job on first return to work after childbirth (%)

Industry	All women*	Returns to job: Full-time	Returns to job: Part-time	Per cent of industry total Full-time	Per cent of industry total Part-time
Food	4.8	5	5	36	64
Textiles, etc.	8.4	13	6	49	51
Engineering	7.7	13	5	54	46
Other Manufacturing	6.3	8	6	41	59
Distribution	18.0	16	19	29	71
Professional and scientific services	21.0	17	23	26	74
Insurance and government	7.8	7	8	30	70
Miscellaneous services	22.5	18	25	25	75
Primary	3.3	3	3	32	68
Total	100	100	100		
N=	3085	997	2088		

*Sample of women with children who have ever returned.

opposite direction. The same trends are visible even when separate age groups are examined (see Appendix Tables A4.2 and A4.3).

One further result worth noting alongside this discussion of industrial mobility and transitions is that the industrial mobility across the first break from work for childbirth is, as we know, a transition from full-time to part-time work for many of these women. We can see this in the figures in Table 5.8. It is perhaps not surprising to be reminded therefore that the movement into service industries, heightened over this period, is also a movement into part-time jobs in service industries. The figures in Table 5.8 show the distribution by industry and by part-time or full-time status of the jobs to which women first return after an experience of childbirth. In total 68 per cent of these first return jobs were part-time jobs. Only a very small proportion of the part-time jobs were in the manufacturing industries; 22 per cent of the total. A higher proportion of full-time jobs, 40 per cent, were in manufacturing. Each one of the industries had some part-time jobs, but the proportions were far higher in the case of the service and distribution industries. An analysis of the transitions according to whether the women returned to a full or part-time job also revealed that women who took up full-time jobs after childbirth were far more likely than those taking part-time jobs to be in the same industry on their return; the difference was most significant in the case of those starting out in manufacturing.

It seems likely therefore that a woman who looks for a part-time job when she is returning to work after childbirth, will get a job in one of the service industries. The overall results undoubtedly arise from the combination of women's preferences for part-time work, manufacturing industry's relative failure to provide part-time jobs (despite the mention of twilight shifts for women), and service industry's plenteous provision of part-time jobs for women.

FIRST JOBS TO MOST RECENT JOBS

The transitions between women's first jobs and their most recent jobs in 1980 are set out in Table 5.9. The figures are provided for each 10-year age group for women with children. In the whole sample of women with children 75 per cent of women who started out in services stayed in services; only 35 per cent of those starting out in the distribution industry were still in it for their most recent job; the value for those remaining in manufacturing was 44 per cent with a similar sized shift – 42 per cent – occurring from manufacturing into services. These figures suggest that for many women, the movement out of manufacturing into services over childbirth is a one-way trip, and their jobs or 'most recent job' after having stopped work for childbirth are far more likely to be jobs in services rather than in manufacturing. The figures are broken down by age in Table 5.9 and they suggest that there may be some slight movement back into manufacturing at a later age; 42 per cent of the over-50s stayed in manufacturing over this transition which is higher than the 36 per cent of the 40–49 age group doing so.

INDUSTRIAL MOBILITY CONCLUSIONS

The main results and conclusions to note from this analysis are as follows. A small group of women remain in one industry throughout

Table 5.9 Industrial mobility between first job and most recent jobs for women with children, by age at interview*

		Most recent job																						
		Age 16-19					Age 20-29					Age 30-39					Age 40-49					Age 50+				
		M	D	S	P	N=	M	D	S	P	N=	M	D	S	P	N=	M	D	S	P	N=	M	D	S	P	N=
												Percentages														
First jobs	M	64	14	21	–	14	52	9	38	1	229	39	12	47	2	427	36	15	49	1	382	42	15	42	1	385
	D	–	100	–	–	6	24	42	32	2	158	19	31	48	3	309	19	31	48	2	236	19	32	49	1	204
	S	20	10	70	–	10	13	11	75	2	251	11	11	75	3	475	10	12	75	3	360	16	15	67	2	371
	P	–	–	–	–	–	18	9	36	36	11	15	15	55	15	20	26	8	35	30	23	23	5	44	28	39

Key: M – Manufacturing industries (1–4)   S – Service industries (6–8)
D – Distribution (5)   P – Primary/Agriculture (19)
*Row percentages sum horizontally to 100%.

their working lives and these have been disproportionately employed in the professional and scientific services. On leaving school, women have entered a range of industries. Women have moved between industries along the lines suggested by their industrial–occupational profiles but there has been a tendency for greater movement to occur from manufacturing to service industries than occurs in the reverse direction from services to manufacturing. These transitions out of manufacturing and into services have received a large boost over the breaks from work taken over childbirth by these women and here the movement is also from full-time to part-time work. There may have been a very slight tendency for women to move back from services into manufacturing towards the end of their work history, but we cannot be sure if this is a trend since we only have one group of women aged over 50 who have reached this late stage of their working lives.

We can now make some more general comments about the relevance of these findings both to Britain's changing industrial structure, and to other studies of the way women's life-cycle industrial mobility fits in with such labour market structures. One hypothesis about the links between life-cycle industrial mobility and the industrial structure has come from Sleeper (1975) who suggested that women enter the labour market through low wage industries like distribution by choice and move subsequently into higher wage industries. This appears to be an erroneous view of women's life-cycle industrial mobility as revealed here. Many of these women (approximately 25 per cent) had a job in the distribution industry upon leaving school, but there is only a small amount of mobility from the distribution to higher wage manufacturing industries subsequently. There is far more mobility from distribution to service industries and the latter are often lower wage industries, at least according to mean earnings figures. Other studies of school leavers' job choices, Dex (1982), have found that young women ended up in the distribution industry occupations largely when they failed to obtain jobs in other occupations they preferred. Sleeper's suggestions do not therefore fit the facts of women's life-cycle industrial mobility.

Neither do other studies, like that of Sleeper, offer a view of life-cycle industrial mobility which fits what we know about the structure of opportunities in Britain. An examination of published earnings figures series in Department of Employment publications over the 1960s and 1970s reveals a certain amount of stability in women's average weekly or average hourly earnings. Firstly, and most notably, the range is very narrow, especially in comparison with the range of men's earnings. It seems highly debatable whether women (or anyone) could distinguish between many of the industrial categories according to earnings levels although there are undoubtedly local and regional variations. There are however differences between manual and non-manual earnings and the ranking of industries according to their earnings varies in these two types of occupation. Within the range of average earnings of industries for manual jobs, some manufacturing industries have had consistently higher earnings than jobs in services. In particular, earnings for women in the transport, vehicles, timber and engineering industries have been higher than those in other manufacturing industries, and higher than earnings in services industries. Earnings in public administration, however, have been higher than those in manufacturing industries like textiles, clothing or food, that is, in the manufacturing industries with higher proportions of women employed in them. So, in the case of women's manual earnings, it is not the case that all manufacturing industries have had higher earnings than all service industries (if we include public administration as a service) but a more complex picture exists. In the case of non-manual earnings, public administration had consistently come top of the ranking, ahead of the range of manufacturing industries which has had textiles at the bottom of the list.

Any attempt to construct a theory about women's life-cycle industrial mobility needs to consider both the elements of industrial structure noted here and the facts of women's lifetime industrial mobility, if a better empirically grounded account is to be offered. What is clear from a range of sources is that women's work takes place in a low wage sector. The movements that occur within that sector are heavily determined by women's occupational attachments combined with the fluctuations and structural changes in the British economy as a whole. Such changes are reflected in women's individual experiences in a number of ways: women have entered the labour market through obtaining jobs in the slightly higher waged manufacturing industries. Since they are young women they have presumably been paid at low rates. This gateway has been declining however since the Second World War. Relatively few women have stayed in the manufacturing sector throughout their working lives. It is more common to find movements between the sectors, but with a tendency to move out of manufacturing into low wage services as women have grown older; women might have expected to gain increases in earnings, had they stayed on in manufacturing. This shift has been particularly marked over the break from work for childbirth when it can also be seen as a move into part-time work as well as an experience of downward occupational mobility for many. The industrial mobility across the break for childbirth is also likely to be a move from higher earnings to lower earnings industries – and this trend would be likely to be emphasised further if earnings from part-time work were compared with earlier full-time earnings – even if hourly rates are being compared.

These results fit better with the idea that women's lower wages – and those of young women in particular – have been used to prop up an ailing and declining British manufacturing sector, providing it with a more graceful and smoother decline than might otherwise have been the case. The decline has been occurring nonetheless as the slightly reduced entry into these jobs illustrates. The move out of manufacturing which women have experienced later in their work history and the relative failure of the manufacturing sector to provide more part-time jobs for women needs however to be explained. There may have been both advantages and restrictions contributing to this trend. The pressure to pay more experienced or older workers higher wages is eliminated if they leave before reaching that age. There may be other advantages to having a new supply of younger workers in physically more demanding jobs in some cases. There may also have been more union opposition to bringing about changes which might have extended women's working opportunities in manufacturing industries. All of these suggestions can be supported from individual industry studies, for example West (1982) and Cavendish (1982). On the other hand, the growth of part-time jobs in services may have resulted in part from there being more freedom to offer jobs suited to women's preferences. A combination of these demand and supply considerations are likely to have contributed to producing these results. It is important to note, nonetheless, that the outcome has relied upon the 'natural' break in women's work history experience for childbirth. There is a sense in which women's individual work history experiences, over the childbirth period in particular, reflect structural changes in the British economy, of a decline in the manufacturing sector and growth in services. There is undoubtedly a parallel story to be found in employers' recruitment policies towards women workers which cannot be explored here.

INDUSTRIAL STRUCTURE

The work history information of women in WES offers other insights into the position of women in Britain's industrial structure. As well as considering women's profiles of industrial movements, as we have done earlier in this chapter, an analysis of women's job tenure and job-leaving reasons by industry, in the aggregate, can reveal elements of women's role in the industrial structure; it is to this analysis that we now turn. In particular, the extent of involuntary job separations can be an important indicator of the demand for women's labour, and of how the demand fluctuates.

Table 5.10   Mean duration of jobs in each industry*

| Industry | Mean duration in months | | |
	All jobs	Full-time jobs only	Part-time jobs only
Food	35.5	36.1	33.5
Textiles, etc.	37.3	37.9	33.9
Engineering	36.6	37.5	32.2
Other manufacturing	34.1	39.4	29.6
Distribution	29.8	29.6	30.5
Professional and scientific services	35.9	35.2	37.4
Insurance and government	34.0	35.4	28.0
Miscellaneous services	30.2	29.3	32.2
Primary	40.1	41.9	37.0

*Jobs which had not ended at the interview were not included. (Including them does not significantly affect the results.)

The mean durations of time women spent in jobs in the various industry categories are displayed in Table 5.10. All the recorded jobs of all the women in the survey are included in these calculations, irrespective of when they were held. The mean durations cover a surprisingly narrow range. The most significant results are that the lowest values are in the distribution industry and in miscellaneous services. Full-time jobs in manufacturing also have a higher mean duration than part-time jobs in manufacturing whereas, on the whole, part-time jobs in services have a higher mean duration than full-time jobs in services. If turnover is an indicator, on the supply side, of workers' dissatisfactions, then these results could be argued to confirm the undesirability of jobs in the distribution industry. Other than the two industries mentioned, there do not appear to be any significant differences in the average durations of jobs between manufacturing or service industries. It is also worth noting that part-time workers did not appear to be necessarily more unstable than full-time workers, especially in service industries or in distribution; these are the two industries which have large proportions of part-time jobs. The figures suggest that there is a large amount of similarity between the turnover of women in different industries; this parallels their similar low range of earnings opportunities.

The main reasons women left their jobs are set out for each industry in Table 5.11, where all jobs left prior to the 1980 interview have been included.[5] From this large array of figures a number of results are worth noting. Very few women leave jobs in any industry with the purpose of going to college, looking after a sick or elderly relative or for 'other' reasons (which includes having been demobbed after the war). Leaving a job to have a child or get married or look after children constitute approximately one quarter of all job leaving reasons and this proportion applies across industries with relatively minor variation. Women seem slightly more likely to leave manufacturing industries for this reason than they leave services, a result which overlaps with the fact that women are less likely to have jobs in manufacturing after childbirth and they are more likely to have jobs in services then.

The largest proportion of job leaving reasons is for dissatisfaction with the job but here again there is variation by industry. Notably, distribution has the largest proportion of jobs left because of dissatisfaction – which confirms the suggestion made earlier, on the basis of the turnover figures, that the distribution industry provides fewer satisfying jobs for women than other industries. The industries with the lowest proportions who leave because of dissatisfaction with their job, or having a better one to go to, are professional and scientific services and engineering. There is other evidence to suggest that these industries might be more satisfactory; the industrial profile analysis showed that women are often more continuously attached to their jobs in the professional and scientific service industries; also, engineering was one of the higher-paying jobs for women. It must be noted, however, that leaving a job because of dissatisfaction is the single largest reason women gave for leaving jobs in every industry, and this reason swamps most of the others in size. Whilst movement between jobs by these women may have some coherence when viewed from the standpoints of either occupational or industrial mobility, these job-leaving reasons suggest that a large amount of that mobility can be

Table 5.11 Percentage of jobs in industry left for following main reasons

Industry	Involuntary Temporary separation	Dissatisfaction/ better job	Illness	To go to college/ education	Pregnant/ Marriage look-after children	Move because of husband's job	Move for other reason	Look after sick elderly relative	Other*	Total† %	N=
Food	6	37	5	1	25	4	6	1	3	100	965
Textiles	2	39	5	1	28	3	5	2	4	100	2113
Engineering	3	36	5	1	29	4	5	1	4	100	1941
Other Manufacturing	4	40	4	1	26	4	6	1	4	100	1783
Distribution	5	47	4	2	20	3	4	1	4	100	4097
Professional & Scientific Services	6	36	5	2	26	8	8	2	3	100	2918
Insurance & government	7	41	3	2	24	5	6	1	6	100	1983
Miscellaneous services	9	40	4	2	20	4	7	1	4	100	4079
Primary	24	25	7	2	22	4	6	1	3	100	440

*'Other' included 'demobbed' after the war.
†Employer changes have been excluded.

viewed as a search for satisfaction in work and a rejection of dissatisfying conditions of one sort or another.

A few other figures in Table 5.11 stand out although they are in the smaller groups. Women in professional and scientific services jobs are more likely to leave their jobs because their husbands changed jobs or because they moved house, possibly at marriage. This result also matches earlier findings that women in semi-professional occupations were more likely to change jobs or leave a job for these reasons, presumably because they are more often married to men with higher socio-economic status, who experience geographical mobility in their work more often. Another more minor result is that jobs in the miscellaneous services industries are more likely to be temporary in nature. Manufacturing industries appear to be slightly more prone either to dismissing women or making them redundant. It is worth making a more extensive examination of involuntary job separations.

The industries from which involuntary job separations occurred are listed in Table 5.12 and the jobs are distinguished there by whether they were full or part-time.[6] Involuntary job separations occurred most frequently in the distribution and miscellaneous service industries, followed by large but less frequent occurrences in textiles and engineering. This ranking of the frequencies was similar in all cases irrespective of whether jobs were full or part time in status. Some of the higher frequencies, however, are clearly caused by women having more jobs in some of these industries. When the effect of some industries' having more job changes is eliminated, by taking involuntary separations as a percentage of all changes in the industry, the results show that manufacturing and distribution industries have the highest frequencies of involuntary separations; the differentials between these and other industries, however, are quite different for part-time and full-time jobs. In the case of full-time jobs, there is only a slightly greater frequency of involuntary job separations in the manufacturing and distribution industries, but for part-time jobs the lead of manufacturing industries over the others is considerable, and distribution has a much lower frequency of these job separations than the manufacturing industries.

Women are far more likely to leave their part-time manufacturing jobs because of dismissals or redundancies than are women in either part-time jobs in other (service) industries or full-time jobs in services or even full-time jobs in manufacturing. The distribution industry is similar to manufacturing industries when full-time jobs are being considered, but not to the same extent when part-time jobs are examined.

Table 5.12 Industries from which involuntary job separations occur

	Part-time jobs		Full-time jobs		Total jobs	
	Per cent involuntary job separations in each industry	Involuntary job separations as a % of all part-time jobs left in each industry	Per cent involuntary job separations in each industry	Involuntary job separations as a % of all full-time jobs left in each industry	Per cent total involuntary separations in each industry	Involuntary job separation as a % of all jobs left in each industry
Food, drink, etc.	6	15	7	11	7	12
Textiles	12	19	16	11	15	12
Engineering	14	23	14	10	14	12
Other manufacturing	10	17	11	9	11	10
Distribution	22	11	22	9	22	9
Professional and scientific	9	5	4	2	5	3
Insurance, public and local govt.	5	7	6	5	6	5
Miscellaneous	21	9	19	8	19	8
Primary/agricultural	1	6	1	6	1	6
Total	100		100		100	
Total number of job changes	501	4614	1233	15705	1734	20319

We might expect the distribution industry's results to lie somewhere between manufacturing and service industries since its prospects are linked to both sectors; and they do. These results are consistent with an analysis of employment changes by industry in Dex and Perry (1984) where women's part-time jobs in manufacturing exhibited the greatest fluctuations over the 1970s decade.

There are obviously differences in job turnover between these industries but the effects of such differences are difficult to predict or eliminate from the results. Higher turnover in some industries, if it occurred for voluntary reasons would perhaps reduce the level of involuntary separations although the higher turnover could also be a result of more involuntary job separation because of the need of certain industries to keep more in tune with the fluctuating economy. The distribution industry is known to have a higher labour turnover than other industries, and to have a very high proportion of its total costs as labour costs. It is not surprising therefore to find it employing large proportions of women (and young people) who are cheaper employees. The results of the analysis of WES women also suggest the distribution industry has a reasonably high frequency of involuntary job separation.

The service industries proper do not experience involuntary job separations as frequently although the comparison is of women's experiences rather than of women in comparison with men. These results do fit with Bruegel's (1979) and Dex and Perry's (1984) results which suggested that women's employment in the service industries has given them some protection from the effects of recent recession, in so far as involuntary job separations are an 'effect of recession'.

It is also possible to construct a time series of women's involuntary job separations and compare their fluctuations with those of the economy as a whole. The occurrence of involuntary job separations in each year from 1948 to 1979 was expressed as a proportion of all the jobs left in that year and plotted as a time series (Figure 5.1). Another way of expressing the frequency of this experience was to calculate the number of involuntary separations as a proportion of the number of women working at any time in that particular year. This series is also plotted on Figure 5.1 and it can be seen to follow the same trend and undulations as the proportion expressed on the base of all jobs. The average yearly values of total unemployment are also displayed alongside the experience of involuntary job separations and the similarities between the changes in unemployment and the total yearly frequency of involuntary separations is quite striking; the general upward trend is visible in both, and many of the fluctuations coincide.

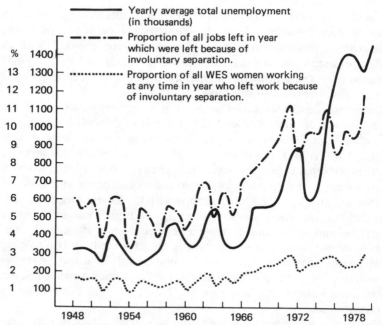

Figure 5.1 Proportion of involuntary job separations and total unemployment

The Pearson correlation coefficients between these variables are 0.77 and 0.74 for the two series and the correlations are both highly significant. These significant values give further evidence of the close correspondence and relationship between levels of total unemployment in the economy and the proportions of women's involuntary job separations. Women's experiences of involuntary job separations appear to be related to fluctuations in the economy as a whole although it is difficult to be more precise here. In so far as it is manufacturing and, in particular, part-time jobs in manufacturing which produce the involuntary separations the results overlap with other studies (Dex and Perry, 1984) to suggest that these women's jobs are part of a highly vulnerable sector of women's labour markets. This theme will be taken up again in Chapter 6.

CONCLUSIONS

This analysis of women's industrial profiles and their industrial mobility has begun to reveal more of the ways in which women's individual work histories tie in with larger-scale changes in Britain's industrial structure. Some of the individual level descriptions may be obvious; for example, the cohort participation rates of women have shown marked increases at ages which must represent post-childbirth working experiences of women, and the growth of women's work in services has also been well documented as has the decline in the manufacturing industries. These results show the extent to which these changes quite clearly rely upon the 'natural' break from work for childbirth experienced by the majority of women; this break also providing both a flow out of manufacturing and a flow into part-time jobs in services. In some cases a change in the classification of the woman's industrial profile resulted.

The implication of this shift for British women is that they experience considerable downward occupational mobility and not much upward occupational mobility across childbirth, predominantly because service sector jobs in Britain are largely part-time jobs. If British women are protected from the effects of recession by being in the growing service sector, they gain that measure of employment security at the expense of their occupational status.

The structure of industry has accommodated to women's work in Britain, although this may be a mixed blessing. British women's movement out of manufacturing and into services over their break from work for childbirth is undoubtedly linked to their supply-side desire for part-time jobs whilst they are bearing the responsibilities of child-rearing. There are demand considerations however since in Britain this process has been occurring whilst men's employment in manufacturing has been declining. In this sense, the seemingly 'natural' turnover of women because of childbirth allows manufacturing industries in Britain to shed their workforce of women without any of the contractual problems which men present. It would not be surprising therefore to see manufacturing industries taking on younger women and maybe even preferring this group of workers to the extent that they may perhaps refuse to employ re-entrant women with children. At any rate, the changing industrial structure of the British economy is highly related to the changing structure of women's life-cycle employment.

A number of features about women's labour markets have also been evident in these results which supplement other studies as well as elaborating women's role in the industrial–occupational structure. We will return to these themes in the final chapter and use these results to offer a more grounded theory of women's labour market segmentation based on their work-history experiences.

6 The Structures of Women's Careers

The analysis of women's work histories from the Women and Employment Survey data has permitted us to see patterns of women's occupational and industrial mobility over their lifetime. The patterns emerge from the combination of women's supply-side preferences and constraints which vary over their life cycle, with the structure of labour market opportunities; the structure has in some cases moulded itself to women's acceptance of childcare responsibilities over family formation through the growth of part-time work. Women's priorities also appear to vary over their life-cycle. In their early years of working, occupational preferences have priority whereas during the family formation period women often trade off their preferred occupation in order to obtain a job with fewer hours. Much downward occupational mobility resulted from women taking part-time jobs after childbirth. The hours of work thus become the main priority, over family formation, superseding occupational preferences, although the latter can come to dominate again in later life. A set of patterns of industrial mobility were also documented which are determined by women's occupational rather than by their industrial choices.

The fact that patterns of occupational choice were visible suggests that it does make sense to think of women having careers. It is not the everyday sense of this term we are using, however, since 'career' as commonly used has a very restricted meaning and would apply, at most, to one or two women's occupations. Women were found to exhibit occupational attachment and preferences in the way they returned to their chosen occupations, even after temporary disruptions and downward occupational mobility. When few women replied in the main WES interview, therefore, that they were working to follow a career, they were not saying that occupational choice was unimportant to them; they were recognising the limited opportunities in many women's occupations; they may have been responding also to their loss of occupational status after taking up a part-time job after childbirth. In the case of women with young children, they were also recognising, no doubt, that their acceptance of being primarily responsible for childcare meant that hours of work took higher priority than a preferred occupation. This is part of the supply-side mechanism by which many women experience downward occupational mobility over childbirth. Women can still see themselves as permanent members of the labour force over this period, however, even though their priorities might change.

A number of other important results and conclusions emerged from these women's work histories. There was a sizeable amount of underachievement for these women as they left school and entered the labour market. Some of the women with A levels were found to obtain only semi-skilled jobs and they went on, in many cases, to have a semi-skilled profile. This underachievement, when combined with the downward occupational mobility which many women experience over the lifetime, constitutes a large amount of wasted talent. The waste results from the combined effects of the household division of labour and the structure of labour market opportunities for women. It is difficult to envisage its being eliminated without there being far more flexible arrangements of working hours from employers; a redistribution of the hours of paid and unpaid work within households; measures for the protection of women's occupational status and more extensive low-cost childcare provisions than exist at present.

The results as a whole highlight the importance of women's first jobs. It was not impossible to experience upward mobility after starting off further down the scale, but in many cases the first job was a gateway into a particular occupational profile; it was certainly far less common, and in some cases impossible to get into a higher grade profile after starting off in a lower level one. Occupational mobility was common nonetheless but often it was downward occupational mobility followed by a recovery of status sometime later. Both the likelihood of downward occupational mobility and any subsequent recovery were related to the origin occupation and teachers retained their status most over their life cycle. The other major source of upward occupational mobility came from women obtaining supervisor's status, usually when they were in full-time jobs. The process of British deindustrialisation was seen to be reflected in women's individual profiles over the 'natural' breaks for childbirth.

These results can be combined with others to elaborate a model of labour market segmentation which is described below. The model builds on women's occupational and industrial profiles as they were revealed in these rare work history data.

LABOUR MARKET SEGMENTATION

Theories of segmented labour markets have been particularly crude as far as women's work has been concerned. The initial theories tended to put women into a single category along with blacks; that is, in the secondary sector. Women's occupational mobility was then restricted to movements between secondary sector jobs. The examination of women's lifetime occupational mobility in Chapter 3 suggests that a more complex structure of market segments exists for women. The basic structure of such a model is displayed in Figure 6.1, based on the WES occupational categories. Had a finer breakdown of occupational categories been available, a more detailed description of labour market segments might well have been possible. It is felt that this outline does capture, however, the broad dimensions of women's position in labour market structures in Britain over the past few decades.

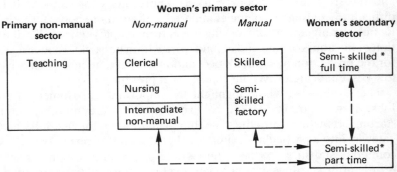

Women's primary sector

| Primary non-manual sector | Non-manual | Manual | Women's secondary sector |

*Semi-skilled includes selling, child care, semi-skilled domestic, other semi-skilled, unskilled and a very few semi-skilled factory or low grade clerical.

Figure 6.1   Labour market segmentation and women's employment

Women can be found, firstly, in the *Primary Non-Manual Sector*, when they have teaching jobs. Women and men share these jobs which have many of the characteristics of primary jobs in the original dual labour market formulation; notably, they have internal labour markets, lower turnover, higher pay and promotion prospects. Women exhibited occupational attachment to jobs in teaching and they have a high chance of retaining their status in teaching after disruptions or over breaks from work for childbirth. We did find some downward mobility out of teaching occurred over women's lifetime work history but it was extremely small in comparison with the amounts of mobility out of other occupations. This sector is therefore fairly autonomous. Its main inflow is from women at the point of leaving full-time education. (Sexual segmentation can still occur within this category, but would only be visible at a very much more micro institutional level; such is not our concern at the moment.) Some types of trained nursing jobs may also be part of this sector.

Women have a primary sector of their own, the *Women's Primary Sector*, which is a sexually segregated sector on the whole. It has two divisions within it, the non-manual occupations of clerical, nursing and intermediate non-manual, and the manual occupations of skilled and semi-skilled factory. All are full-time jobs. Women exhibit attachments to their occupations in all of the women's primary sector occupations. On the whole, there is little movement between occupations in each sub-group; clerical workers tend to stay in clerical work, for example, and semi-skilled factory workers stay in semi-skilled factory work. As well as a lack of mobility, the two sub-sectors are also distinguishable according to their pay, their conditions of work and their job-leaving reasons, as noted in Chapter 3. Women's non-manual occupations have higher pay than the manual ones (Joshi, 1984), and women are less likely to leave these non-manual jobs because of ill-health or redundancy; they are more likely to experience disruptions from husband's job changes however. When mobility does occur, the movement is largely out of full-time occupations, either non-manual or manual, into the part-time area of the *Women's Secondary Sector*. Some return mobility takes place, and these women return to their former occupations in the women's primary sector; it is by no means all women who recover their status after a move into the part-time secondary sector. In fact, for the majority who move, the trip is one-way and they then stay on in the secondary sector.

The *Women's Secondary Sector* contains the occupations which constitute the semi-skilled profile: selling; child-care; semi-skilled domestic; other semi-skilled; unskilled and some cases of semi-skilled factory and low level clerical work. It is a sexually segregated sector with two divisions; one is a sub-sector of full-time jobs and the other a sector of part-time jobs. Part-time jobs are not necessarily higher turnover jobs however, particularly when in service industries. The part-time and full-time jobs are largely in the same occupations with similar amounts of sexual segregation although, again, the sub-sectors are distinguishable because the part-time jobs have lower rates of pay, worse conditions of service and fewer benefits than the full-time jobs. Movement occurs between the full-time and part-time sectors; most of the movement is into part-time largely over women's break from work for childbirth. In this way, the part-time sector is one which is formed to coincide with life-cycle variations in women's employment. Some women return to full-time jobs later. The part-time women's secondary sector also receives an inflow from the women's primary sector, as described above, and some movement occurs in the reverse direction. The vast majority of job changes which are initiated in this sector, however, are transitions to other jobs within the same sector. There is some evidence that the part-time sector, especially when the jobs are in manufacturing industries, are more subject to fluctuations in line with the business cycle operating in the whole economy (Dex and Perry, 1984).

We have documented the broad outlines of labour market segmentation for women's employment. On the basis of women's work histories, it has been possible to identify sectors and sub-sectors and the mobility channels between them. This schema could well be refined if a more detailed classification of occupations were available. A better classification of nursing jobs may well put trained nurses firmly in the primary non-manual sector for example. It is also worth noting that women seem to be aware of a ranking of these sectors which puts primary non-manual at the top of the list and women's secondary sector jobs at the bottom. Their choices, from leaving school onwards reflect this ranking, and the occupational profiles identified earlier result largely when women are successful in the. pursuit of their preferences. Semi-skilled profiles probably result more from the failure to successfully achieve their occupational choices.

The model of occupational labour market segmentation overlaps with an industrial structure to some extent. In the structure of industry segmentation as set out in Figure 6.2, the primary non-manual sector

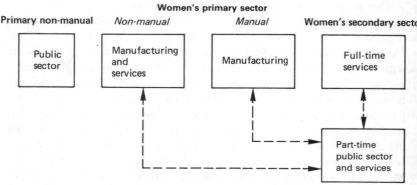

Figure 6.2   Industrial segmentation and women's employment

is largely one of public sector jobs for women. The women's primary sector (manual) contains many of the manufacturing sector jobs for women. On the whole, these manufacturing jobs are in industries which are declining or facing stringent competition. The process of deindustrialisation, as it is reflected in women's work histories occurs along the transition from the women's primary sector (manual) to the women's part-time secondary sector; the latter consists mainly of public sector and service industry jobs. The women's primary non-manual sector contains jobs in a range of industries although probably more in services than in manufacturing, and the women's secondary sector is likely to be almost wholly jobs in services, with some in the public sector.

We can note some interactions which are likely to have been occurring between women's supply decisions and the industrial structure. In the search for explanations of women's position in the industrial structure, writers seem agreed that there is a link between the growth of domestic appliances, demographic factors which mean that women have finished childbirth and child-rearing earlier and women's employment outside the home (Anthias, 1980; Power, 1983). Women have been drawn into the labour market at the same time that manufacturing production has wanted to sell more domestic durable goods like washing machines. Women's employment has provided a rationale for the purchase of such goods and it has also given many women more control over the household resources, which can be used to purchase these consumer durables. Women have been integrally involved therefore in the process Gershuny (1978, 1983) describes of switching from personal services to the self-service economy of consumer durable goods.

When women have been working in manufacturing industries at cheaper wage rates, they have been supporting, in Britain, an ailing manufacturing sector, allowing it to limp along and be slightly more on a par with the cheap labour production of developing countries in textiles and clothing. Given that productivity gains have been restricted in service industries, then women are also the obvious choice of workers to try and keep down costs in these industries. Mallier and Rosser (1980) have suggested that the growth in part-time work is largely a demand-induced phenomenon. There can be a variety of reasons for employers' preferring part-time work, as Rubery and Tarling (1983) note. Where part-time work is part of the structure of the job because of peak periods or anti-social hours, women are the 'ideal' solution since they are pleased to work part-time. Often the part-time hours coincide with children being at school, or husbands being at home to look after children. The growth in part-time jobs in the public sector has strong links with the lack of formal or statutory child-care or its high cost relative to women's wages. Part-time work can also be a way of employers' coping with vulnerability to business-cycle fluctuations and keeping labour costs to a minimum. Beechey and Perkins's (1983) study of part-time work in Coventry suggested that flexibility was the keynote to understanding employers' demands for part-time workers, in manufacturing, services and the public sector. They also found that employers had ways of meeting their requirements which involved gender distinctions. Women's preference for part-time work, given their child-care responsibilities again make them a highly suitable workforce.

The recent Women and Employment Survey in Britain supported these conclusions by demonstrating that there was a large peak in women's part-time hours at sixteen hours per week, after which employers become liable for more overhead costs associated with women's work. Also, the vast majority of child-care arrangements made by working women involved support from the husband, older children and other relatives. A comparative study of Britain and the USA revealed that the two countries were quite different in this respect; in the USA far more women work full-time and pay for child-care (Dex and Shaw, 1986). One suspects that women's preference for part-time work in Britain could easily change in an environment where the child-care facilities were better and more acceptable than in the 1970s. Employers use of the part-time option in Britain might change if women's preferences were for full-time work but the same advantage of employing women would apply if their labour remained cheaper. One might predict, on these grounds, that as women work more and longer and demand and obtain equal pay, as they are doing, and obtain better child-care, the nature of the industrial distribution of men's and women's work would change alongside these changes. Women have played an active role in bringing about these changes by desiring to purchase new consumer goods, by desiring to have greater control over family resources and their own independent means, by preferring in Britain part-time jobs in order to be able to satisfy their list of desires, described above alongside shouldering domestic responsibilities. In one sense women have succumbed to the persuasive advertising encouraging them to want new consumer durables, which have become the backbone of modern industrial production. These products are not so obviously labour-saving in a direct way (although it is claimed that they are), but women have nevertheless made significant increases in their standard of living, and they have worked hard, doubly hard, to achieve these increases. It is difficult to assess the size of women's influence on the moves towards a self-service economy, without a thorough examination of this issue, but it is undoubtedly great, and possibly the main impetus moving the economy in this direction. At any rate, women's role in the changing industrial structure cannot be over-emphasised just now.

CLASS ANALYSIS

These results also have implications for the debates about women's role in class analysis outlined in Chapter 2. If women are permanently attached to the labour force, with recognisable occupational profiles, a classification of their occupational status is possible, irrespective of whether they happen to be employed at the time or not. Such a classification would need to be established with care and with a recognition that there are strong life-cycle variations in women's occupational positions. This classification could then be used as one indicator amongst others of the status of a household, or the life chances of household members and children in particular. In so far as class analysis has wanted to document the dimensions of inequality in society, women's employment records and whether a household has one or two earners etc. are important indicators of that inequality; they should not be neglected. The identification of women's occupational profiles has opened up a route through which households can be examined in which men and women have different or similar occupational statuses. The availability of men's employment histories would obviously be a valuable addition to such analyses.

In so far as some authors have suggested that the focus of class analysis should concentrate on social relations within households, women's occupational mobility as described here is also of relevance. Walby (1984), for example, argued that housewives and husbands are classes; also that both full and part-time housewives are classes. Single women in paid employment should take their class position from their own occupation. Married women have a dual class position; one from their paid work and one as a housewife in relation to their husband. Critics might argue in reply that this apparent changing of class status over a life-cycle offends against their notion of class which has at its basis the idea of continuity. This is not necessarily a problem however Women's class position from their labour market status may well remain fairly constant as revealed by their profile classification. On the other hand, it seems quite appropriate to consider class as a concept applying to certain relationships, for example, those within the workplace or within marriage, with individuals being allowed to move in and out of them over their lifetime. There will, of course, be very definite material consequences of moving in and out of either marriage or employment which will be relevant to the structure of inequality class analysis is attempting to capture.

The availability of women's work history experiences has provided the valuable opportunity to explore these issues and document more of the labour market structures which contributed to their formation It is to be hoped that men's work histories will become available in the near future, on the same scale, so that we can begin to complete the picture.

Appendix 1 The Women and Employment Survey

The Women and Employment Survey consisted of single interviews with 5588 women between the ages of 16 and 59 between April and June of 1980. The sample was obtained by approaching a national random sample of addresses and interviewing all the women at each address. The sample details and response rates are described in Martin and Roberts (1984). The main interview schedule collected information about women's education, training and current employment status, their family and household circumstances, their husband's education and employment status, their attitudes and their work history experiences over the previous two years. In addition a work history schedule was administered to most of these women (5320) which recorded systematically, on the basis of a memory recall, their working and not-working periods after leaving school up until the interview. It has become usual in social sciences to use the term 'work' to refer to activity which may or may not be paid, with 'employment' being used to signify paid work. This survey used the term work in its everyday sense to mean paid work, for reasons given in Martin and Roberts (1984) and the same terminology is used throughout this volume.

The analysis undertaken and reported here concentrates on using the information in the work history schedule in conjunction with some of the information contained in the main schedule. The structure and terminology of the work history schedule needs to be grasped in order to understand the analysis which took place, since this structure provides the limits and constraints within which the analysis had to take place.

Women in the sample were asked to give an outline structure of their work history from leaving full-time education onwards, in terms of periods of working full time, working part time, not working and being in full-time education. The dates at which transitions took place between any of these types of activities was recorded. For purposes of this survey 'a period' had to span the duration of at least one month in order to be recorded. Working periods and not-working periods are therefore recorded to the nearest month. The interviewer was told to return, after outlining this basic structure, to the beginning of the work history and ask for further details about each period.

When the period was one of full or part-time work, women were asked about the jobs they had held within a working period, and the occupation, industry, supervisor's status, reason for leaving and duration of each job were recorded. The most important feature to grasp about this procedure is that a 'working period' is one in which a number of jobs can be held and it could even cover experiences of unemployment so long as they lasted less than one month. A restricted range of occupational (12) and industrial (9) classifications were used to classify women's jobs.

131

In the case of a not-working period, women were asked about their reasons and also their main reason for not working over the whole period. These reasons provide some information about whether women were economically active, although not working, but no attempt was made to classify not-working periods, according to whether they were economically active or not. When a woman had started work again, at the end of the period of not working, she was asked why she had started work. Women were presented with a range of precoded answers in each case, and these had been determined after the pilot stage of the survey.

This systematic recording of working and not-working periods was combined with a series of life events of these women recorded in the main interview schedule. In particular, it was possible to see women's working activity alongside their marriage dates, their births of children, adoptions or deaths of children, and their ends of marriages (that is, death or divorce). This mixture of life events, working and not-working experiences, reasons for leaving jobs and reasons for not working provided a very rich data source about these women's longitudinal experiences. The fact that this information was based on women's memories may raise certain questions about its accuracy. The OPCS/DE Report of this survey discusses this issue and provides reassuring details about the tests which were carried out. There is cross-checking information contained in questions within the interview schedule. Their warning does apply however, that 'some caution should be attached to the interpretation of retrospective information' (Martin and Roberts, 1984).

Appendix 2 Occupational Mobility in the Aggregate

The number of different occupations held by the women in this survey is outlined in Table A2.1 for the whole sample sub-divided by age, and for a further two sub-groups: women with children and childless women. The majority of women have either one or two occupations throughout their working lives although there is some variation by age. Alternatively, one could say that more than 50 per cent of each age group have at least one change of occupation, and the figure is 80 per cent for the over 50s. We need to remember, however, that these are not necessarily vertical occupational moves. At least three of the occupations in the list of categories used in this survey were semi-skilled so that movement between them, whilst being recorded as occupational changes, are not exactly vertical occupational movements. It is perhaps not so surprising that the number of occupations increases with age – which presumably represents, in the majority of cases, women's working experience. The possibility of changing one's occupation obviously increases the longer one works, however, these figures are not necessarily wholly the result of experience–age effects. The older generations could have been an occupationally more mobile workforce; alternatively, were the workforce divided into mobile and stable workers (which might have links with certain occupations) and the frequency of mobile workers had decreased over time – again this apparent 'age' effect would be seen in the aggregate results. We cannot be sure therefore of what causes this apparent increase in occupational mobility at this stage.

The figures in Table A2.1 do show, however, that women with children have more occupational changes than childless women of the same age, and again the trend for increased occupational mobility with age can be discerned in these sub-groups. Thus, at the aggregate level, these results support the idea that occupational change occurs as a result of breaks from working to have children, although we cannot say from these figures whether it is downward occupational mobility that occurs.

We can see more of the type of occupational movements represented in Table A2.1 by examining, again in the aggregate, as a summary, the cross tabulations of origin occupation to destination occupation movements, as outlined in Table A2.2. The figures show, for all job changes which take place, the percentage of all job changes which stay in the same occupational group, in comparison with those which end up in a different occupational group. Summing the percentages horizontally across each row gives 100 per cent and the frequencies of jobs in each of the origin occupations is tabulated at the end of each row. The diagonal percentages reveal the percentage of job changes that remain in the same occupational group.

The highest diagonal percentages are in the teacher, professional, nursing

Table A2.1 Number of different occupations

Number of different occupations	Percent with number of occupations by age										
	All women					Women with children			Childless		
	16–19	20–29	30–39	40–49	50–59	30–39	40–49	50–59	30–39	40–49	50–59
1	69	45	34	27	21	32	25	19	46	37	31
2	25	32	31	30	29	31	29	28	32	34	36
3	6	16	22	25	26	23	26	27	16	15	19
4	—	5	9	13	17	9	13	17	5	9	12
5 or more	—	2	4	6	7	4	6	8	1	5	1
Total	100	100	100	100	100	100	100	100	100	100	100
$N =$	303	1232	1410	1135	1157	1235	1003	1004	175	132	153
Range =	1–4	1–7	1–7	1–9	1–8	1–7	1–9	1–8	1–5	1–6	1–5
No working experience N	34	26	6	5	11	6	5	11	—	—	—

Table A2.2 Origin occupation compared with destination occupation of all job changes for all women in this survey

Origin occupation	Professional	Teacher	Nurse	Intermediate non-manual	Clerical	Skilled	Shop Assistant	Child-care	Semi-skilled Factory	Semi-skilled Domestic	Other semi-skilled	Unskilled	Total [%]	Number of jobs in origin occupation
													Destination occupation	
Professional	78	4	6	2	4	2	3	—	—	—	—	—	100	95
Teacher	—	85	2	1	4	2	2	1	1	1	—	—	100	609
Nurse	—	2	71	1	8	2	5	2	2	5	1	1	100	1125
Intermediate non-manual	1	3	2	50	21	3	8	1	3	5	2	2	100	488
Clerical	—	1	2	3	73	2	7	1	3	4	2	1	100	5961
Skilled	—	—	3	2	10	45	11	1	13	7	3	5	100	1444
Shop Assistant	—	—	3	3	17	4	42	1	14	8	4	4	100	2982
Child-care	—	1	9	1	14	5	10	26	12	13	3	5	100	347
Semi-skilled Factory	—	—	1	—	5	4	10	1	57	9	5	7	100	4085
Semi-skilled Domestic	—	1	3	1	9	7	11	2	17	38	4	8	100	1600
Other semi-skilled	—	1	2	2	9	5	11	2	20	10	31	8	100	912
Unskilled	—	—	1	1	6	7	9	2	23	17	5	28	100	52
														20405

Numbers include some unclassified occupations not displayed in table.

and clerical occupations. In these occupations, 71 per cent or more of job changes are into the same occupation, reaching its highest percentage of 85 per cent in teaching. There is a tendency for job changes to be more frequently into other occupations as one moves down the occupational hierarchy with one exception. Women starting off in semi-skilled factory jobs, at any particular time, are far more likely than those in other semi-skilled occupations to move to another semi-skilled factory job; 57 per cent of all job changes which originate in semi-skilled factory jobs end in this occupation. The diagonal proportions for the other occupations are much lower, largely around 26 to 40 per cent and they are at their lowest in unskilled and child-care occupations. This aggregate picture fits neatly with the description of profiles already offered. The occupations where people remain despite job changing, were clerical, semi-skilled factory and the semi-professional jobs – and the higher diagonal elements for these occupations are what we would expect. Women were found to move much more between semi-skilled jobs and this too is reflected in the lower diagonal elements for these semi-skilled occupations as well as in the higher proportions in the off-diagonal transitions into other semi-skilled jobs. It is perhaps worth noting here that the child-care occupation has much in common with other semi-skilled work in this respect.

Some further observations can be made about the mobility between occupations. The most predominant moves out of semi-skilled occupations are into other semi-skilled occupations, but there are large percentages moving into unskilled jobs from these occupations – unskilled work constitutes the only downward occupational move from semi-skilled work. Few if any of the higher-grade non-manual occupations move directly into unskilled work. In addition, there are small but noticeable movements up the scale from semi-skilled occupations into nursing, clerical and even into teaching. Some of the movement into clerical work probably constitutes a horizontal move from semi-skilled work, as described in the semi-skilled profile, and it results from a broad classification which does not distinguish between the different grades of clerical work. Some of this movement, however, along with movements into nursing and teaching from semi-skilled work, is likely to be women recovering their earlier status after a downward occupational move, following an interruption or childbirth. The off-diagonal elements of the non-manual origin occupations illustrate that downward mobility does occur into manual and semi-skilled jobs and whilst this aggregate table does not illustrate the sequence of these transitions, the earlier descriptions of occupational profiles do point us towards this sort of interpretation.

An examination of the percentages which appear in the vertical destination columns perceives that some occupations are more frequently destination occupations; women move into these to a greater extent than they move into others. We can tell this by the larger percentages appearing in a number of cells in the column; clerical work, shop assistant, semi-skilled factory and semi-skilled domestic occupations, are more predominantly destination occupations than the others. They gain this status through a mixture of upward, downward and horizontal moves, and it is difficult to quantify the importance of the different types, although we can again note that these destination occupations fit in with the women's occupational profiles described in Chapter 3.

Appendix 3 Industrial Mobility in the Aggregate

We can examine the whole set of changes between industries of these women in aggregate. These are displayed in Table A3.1 using all nine industrial categories and then in Table A3.2 where service industries have been grouped into a sector as have manufacturing industries.

The diagonal elements in both tables illustrate the number of changes between industries which start and end in the same industry, as a proportion of all changes which start in that (origin) industry. Without exception, these diagonal percentages are the largest numbers in each row and this illustrates that there is also a large measure of attachment to single industries in women's experiences; that they are quite likely to obtain their new job in the same industry as their old one. Local labour market conditions, where some industries will dominate local employment opportunities, are undoubtedly partly responsible for this attachment. (It would be interesting to compare this picture with that of a similar group of men to see how far women's attachment to industries is similar or different. Unfortunately Sleeper's (1975) research on the industrial mobility of men and women does not provide this information either.)

Some industries have higher diagonal elements than others indicating that women are more likely to move to another job in that industry having already had one. The professional and scientific services are most likely to provide continuing employment, with 63 per cent of job changes which originated in this industry also ending up there. This high value is the parallel industry figure for the high occupational attachment, seen earlier, to teaching and to a lesser extent, to nursing occupations. The distribution, other services and textile industries have the next highest diagonal elements with around 42–44 per cent of changes remaining in the same industries. These values are much lower, however, than those for professional and scientific services and much closer to the other industries. The food industry stands out for having the lowest industrial attachment and interestingly, this industry has had consistently higher turnover rates than other manufacturing industries in the published Department of Employment turnover rate series for manufacturing industries – for women.

The more aggregate Table A3.2 illustrates that there is a very high degree of attachment to service industries in general, with women continuing to be employed in these three service groups even though they change their jobs. Also, 56 per cent of changes starting out from one of the manufacturing industries end up in one of them.

The off-diagonal elements in each table illustrate the changes between different industries and there are few patterns upon which to comment in this complex array of industrial changes. Movements into agriculture are very

137

Table A3.1 Industry by industry changes for all jobs of all WES women

Origin Industry	Food	Textiles	Engineering	Other Manufacturing	Distri-bution	Professional & Scientific Services	Insurance & Govt.	Other Services	Primary	Total [%]	N
					Destination Industry						
	Percent of origin industry which arrive in destination industry indicated										
Food	25	8	11	10	13	10	5	16	2	100	952
Textiles	4	42	8	9	12	7	4	12	1	100	2047
Engineering	5	6	32	10	14	8	9	15	2	100	1899
Other manufacturing	5	7	13	27	13	10	8	16	2	100	1724
Distribution	4	5	8	6	44	9	8	16	1	100	4130
Professional & Scientific services	2	2	4	4	7	63	7	12	1	100	3167
Insurance & Government	2	3	7	6	14	14	37	16	1	100	1999
Other services	3	4	7	6	14	12	9	44	–	100	4028
Primary	5	4	6	4	12	8	5	16	39	100	452

Table A3.2   Industry by industry changes by broad industry group – for all jobs of all WES women

Origin industry	Destination industry				Total [%]	N
	Manufacturing industries	Distribution	Service industries	Primary		

Percent (rounded) of origin industry which arrive in destination industry

Origin industry	Manufacturing industries	Distribution	Service industries	Primary	Total [%]	N
Manufacturing industries	56	13	30	2	100	6622
Distribution	22	44	33	1	100	4130
Service industries	16	11	71	1	100	9194
Primary	20	12	30	39	100	452

Table A3.3   Frequencies of WES sample with one industry only over whole work history until interview

Industry	Age group at interview (%)					
	All ages	16–19	20–29	30–39	40–49	50–59
Food	2	4	2	2	2	4
Textiles, etc.	10	10	9	9	13	12
Engineering	6	6	7	4	5	9
Other manufacturing	6	7	6	7	4	4
Distribution	19	25	20	16	20	13
Professional and scientific services	29	9	25	42	37	31
Insurance and government	12	16	18	7	6	10
Other services	13	22	12	11	10	12
Primary	2	1	1	1	4	6
Total %	100	100	100	100	100	100
N =	1252	189	411	299	189	164
Percentage of whole age group (ever worked) with only one industry	24	63	33	21	17	14

small, as we might expect. Movements into the food and textile industries are also smaller than movements into service industries. The more aggregate figures in Table A3.2 confirm that there is more movement from manufacturing to services than there is from services into manufacturing industries. Two industrial categories stand out as being more likely than other categories to be destination industries; these are other services and to a lesser extent the distribution industry. Women appear to be more likely to move into these two industries than they do into others.

Some of these WES women remained in one industry throughout their work history – at least, they had done so up until the interview. The figures in Table A3.3 indicate that 24 per cent of the whole sample had this experience. This proportion varied considerably with age, however, declining markedly from 63 per cent in the youngest age group (16–19) to only 14 per cent of those aged 50 or over. Thus the likelihood of a woman at the end of her work history being in the same industry as the one she started out in on leaving school is quite small – although even 14 per cent is perhaps larger than we might expect. The distribution by industry of these one-industry experiences illustrates that professional and scientific services accounts for approximately one-third of this group – which is a far higher proportion than occurs for this industry in the distribution of all the jobs of the women in this sample, or of jobs at any particular cross-section. Jobs in the distribution industry also account for a large proportion – around one fifth. Thus, a change of industry, at least once, seems to be the norm for these women and as we have seen already in the case of the professional and scientific services industry (and its associated occupations in teaching and nursing), there is a large measure of occupational attachment, and its associated industrial attachment.

Appendix 4

Table A4.1 Industry of first jobs grouped, by age at interview

Industry group	*16–19*	*20–24*	*25–29*	*30–34*	*35–39*	*40–44*	*45–49*	*50–54*	*55+*
				Percentages					
Manufacturing	29	26	31	33	37	37	37	38	41
Distribution	26	26	22	25	24	24	24	22	18
Services	43	46	46	42	38	36	36	37	38
Agricultural/ primary	1	1	1	1	2	2	2	4	4
Total	100	100	100	100	100	100	100	100	100
N =	303	564	668	762	648	584	551	564	593
classification not available	1	1	—	—	2	2	2	1	3

Table A4.2 Industrial mobility between selected points by age at interview*

Percentages
Last job before 1st birth

First Jobs	Age 20–29					Age 30–39					Age 40–49					Age 50+				
	M	D	S	P	N =	M	D	S	P	N =	M	D	S	P	N =	M	D	S	P	N =
M	66	12	21	—	225	65	9	25	1	418	69	10	20	—	374	71	10	18	1	376
D	28	47	23	1	156	29	44	27	1	306	32	42	25	1	232	27	38	32	3	201
S	14	10	75	2	243	15	9	74	2	471	15	11	72	3	354	22	9	65	4	361
P	18	48	9	54	11	40	20	15	25	20	17	4	35	44	23	11	5	34	50	38

Key: M – manufacturing industries (1–4)   S – service industries (6–8)
     D – distribution (5)   P – primary/agriculture (9)

*Row percentages sum horizontally to 100%.

Table A4.3 Industrial mobility over childbirth by age at interview*

		First Job after birth																			
		Age 20–29					*Age 30–39*					*Age 40–49*					*Age 50+*				
		M	*D*	*S*	*P*	*N =*	*M*	*D*	*S*	*P*	*N =*	*M*	*D*	*S*	*P*	*N =*	*M*	*D*	*S*	*P*	*N =*
Last Job	M	49	10	40	1	121	48	13	36	4	343	49	12	35	3	354	48	16	34	2	364
Before	D	25	34	40	2	68	18	36	44	2	187	10	44	44	3	158	15	43	41	2	131
First	S	11	11	78	1	133	10	14	75	2	398	11	12	75	2	346	15	15	68	2	325
Birth	P	29	1	1	71	7	6	6	50	38	16	11	11	33	44	18	9	9	21	61	33

Key: *M* — Manufacturing industries (1–4) *S* — Service industries (6–8)
D — Distribution (5) *P* — Primary/agriculture (9)

*Row percentages sum horizontally to 100%.

Notes and References

1. Introduction

1. For example, the National Training Survey contained employment records for women and men over a ten-year period.
2. Contributions to the methods of analysing longitudinal data which emerged from this research are described in Dex (1984a).

2. The Distributions of Women's Employment

1. See EOC (1984, table 3.3, p. 77, and table 3.4, p. 78) for sources of these figures.
2. Source is the Women and Employment Survey, Martin and Roberts (1984, table 3.2).
3. Source is New Earnings survey – see EOC (1984, p. 82).
4. Another group of American economists began writing in the 1960s about the same issues calling themselves 'radical economists'. These writers also adopted the concept of a segmented labour market as part of a more radical political economy or class analysis of the USA (Edwards, Reich and Gordon, 1975). Whilst there is a need to recognise some distinctions between the institutional and radical schools, it is convenient to discuss concurrently the value of their shared notion of a segmented labour market since the overlaps are greater than the differences. The specific contribution of radicals is discussed under the section on class analysis.
5. E.g. Bibb and Form (1977), Beck *et al.* (1978) and a review by Sorensen (1983).
6. For a review of this material see Dex (1985, chapter 6).
7. This is not to say that American writers are therefore excluded. American class theorists like E. O. Wright are regarded as being in the European tradition for example.
8. Goldthorpe (1983, p. 470) says that he would alter his view of 'the extent and nature of female participation in the labour market is now such that in the more "normal" conjugal family it is increasingly hard to say whether husband or wife could better be regarded as the family "head" or that in many cases there are in effect two "heads" with, quite often, different class positions'.
9. Walby (1985, pp. 20–1) says: 'From neoclassical economists ... I would take the analysis of the sexual division of labour within and outside the family as a proper subject of study, and the necessity of the analysis of the relation between women's paid and unpaid work ... From Bergmann I would take the analysis of the dismal effects that the crowding of women and blacks into a few occupations has on the market power of these groups ... From Matthaei I would take the necessity for a historical

144

analysis of the development of the sexual division of labour ... From segmented labour market theories like Gordon, Edwards and Reich I would take their focus on the development of segmented labour markets over time through social struggle ... From Hartmann I would take her approach to gender relations in terms of the intersection of patriarchy and capitalism, although I would emphasise the tension between the two systems to a greater extent than she does, and pay greater attention to the reasons for variations in segregation.'

3. Occupational Profiles

1. The National Training Survey preceded the Women and Employment Survey and contained information on women's (and men's) work histories over a ten-year period (see Elias and Main, 1982; Stewart and Greenhalgh, 1982, 1984). There are a number of longitudinal sources of women's work history data in the USA, e.g. National Longitudinal Surveys (see Dex and Shaw, 1986).

2. Goldthorpe (1980, p. 140) says 'It is true that our findings would suggest that certain relatively well-defined types of work life "trajectory" could be specified, but whether it would be possible to assimilate the mobility experience of the population at large to some manageable number of such types is a question which here at least we must leave in doubt'.

3. The instructions given to the interviewers on the classification of occupations was as follows:
   You should code the occupations of all women's jobs recorded during the interview (i.e. Qns. 9(a), 10(a), 76, 108, 113, 147(b) and E on the work history), and the industry of jobs at Qns, 9(b), 10(b) and D on the work history.
   Do not attempt to code during the interview, but make sure you are familiar with the coding frames so that you collect the appropriate information to code during your checking time.
   If you are in doubt about how to code DO NOT ENTER A CODE IN THE BOX – leave it blank and make a note of possible code(s) at the side of the box.
   If an informant does a job which falls into more than one occupation code, code the occupation she spends most time on.
   Similarly if the organisation she works for falls into more than one industry code, code the main one. If the informant's own occupation only relates to one industry code give priority to that code. (e.g. Informant works in a filling station which has a shop attached – if her work is mainly selling petrol, code 08 for industry; if she is mainly in the shop, code 05.)
   Note that anyone who is a trainee is coded to the same occupation as if they had completed the training.

4. In a few cases in this sample teachers were employed in agricultural and primary industries. The occupational profiles of these women differed from the ones described above for public sector (or professional and scientific industries) teachers. These agriculture teachers did not

continue as teachers for very much of their work history, possibly because they were more vulnerable. Nurses were employed in the private sector to a greater extent, especially in their later work profile.

5. This percentage is based on the experience of older women only, who had completed most of their work histories.

6. 'Textiles' here is used to represent the industrial category used in this survey which aggregated textiles, clothing, footwear and leather industries.

7. The article by Coyle (1982) contains information about the job histories of the women in her sample almost unconsciously; she says, 'The industry employs a lot of married women but they tend to be women who have worked in the industry for many years' (p. 17). I take this to mean that they have a semi-skilled factory profile over their working lives.

8. It is in cases like these where one suspects that the occupational classification may not be adequate to distinguish all types of occupational experience. The experience of clerical work in this profile is vastly different from in the clerical profile and it may be a different type of clerical work, unrecognisable because of the single occupational category. Occasionally, jobs in nursing and skilled work were found amidst jobs in the other categories. These are very infrequent and in the case of nursing it seems likely that these were the more semi-skilled nursing auxiliary jobs.

9. Coyle (1984, pp. 102–3) for example describes the occupational choices and advice received by two young women: 'They kept asking you what you'd like to do and they kept saying wouldn't you like to work in a factory, and I ended up in a factory'; 'I thought of being a model. I was a beauty queen you see, but my mum wouldn't let me. I'll stay in tailoring now, the money's good.'

10. McRae (1986) has begun to document the life-style and other characteristics of more extreme cases of women having higher occupations than their husbands, but there is a lot of work needed to be done on the less extreme cases in order to find out whether differences exist between the various categories of households. The ESRC Social and Economic Life Initiative will help to answer these questions.

4. Occupational Mobility

1. Sandell and Shapiro (1978) and Corcoran and Duncan (1979) estimated that only 25 to 30 per cent of the earnings gap could be accounted for by work history differences.

2. Excluding women from the 50–59 age group whose experience of downward occupational mobility (71 women) was a result of being demobbed at the end of the war reduced the frequency in the total sample of this age group from 61 per cent to 55 per cent.

3. Looking-after-home has been grouped together with the more obvious childbearing reasons for leaving a job since it was often given as a reason for leaving jobs over the childbearing phase even when a birth followed.

4. Some of the movements may be horizontal between clerical and semi-skilled jobs – but there is no reason to expect that these spurious

'vertical' moves were more frequent across childrearing breaks than at other times.

5. Killingsworth (1983) discusses the problems of sample selection biases and their effects on the sizes of correlation coefficients.
6. The missing dummy variable from this list of occupations is semi-skilled factory.
7. The highest qualification category, A-levels or above, was omitted since it was highly correlated with the occupational categories like teaching and nursing.
8. See Pindyck and Rubinfeld (1976) for a description of logit regression.
9. Joshi (1985) estimated the costs of women of having children.

5. Industrial Profiles and Industrial Mobility

1. This type of profile may well be the experience of a much larger proportion of the population of British women in so far as it can represent all farmers' wives – although they may not always see themselves as employed in the normal sense.
2. In a few cases nurses who moved between the public and private sector as nurses had a 'services' profile.
3. See Sleeper (1975) for references to these views.
4. A study of 1971 black and white school leavers by Dex (1982) found that individuals ended up with jobs in the distribution industry when they had failed to get their preferred job choice.
5. There is obviously more than one job per person in most cases. Women were asked for their reasons for leaving and these were multicoded. They were also asked for their main reason for leaving. It is only these 'main reasons' which have been included in this analysis.
6. We are including here leaving a job either because of redundancy or dismissal.

Bibliography

ACKER, J. (1980) 'Women and stratification: a review of recent literature' in *Contemporary Sociology*, vol. 9.

ALLEN, S. (1982) 'Gender, inequality and class formation' in A. Giddens ans G., Mackenzie (eds) *Social Class and the Division of Labour*, (Cambridge University Press).

ANTHIAS, F. (1980) 'Women and the reserve army of labour: a critique of Veronica Beechey' in *Capital and Class* 10.

ARMSTRONG, P. (1982) 'If it's only women it doesn't matter so much' in J. West ed.

BACON, R. and W. A. ELTIS (1976) *Britain's Economic Problem: Too Few Producers*, (London: Macmillan).

BARRON, R. D. and G. M. NORRIS (1976) 'Sexual divisions and the dual labour market' in D. L. Barker and S. Allen (eds) *Dependence and Exploitation in Work and Marriage* (London: Longman).

BECK, E. M., P. M. HORAN and C. M. TOLBERT (1978) 'Stratification in a dual economy: a sectoral model of earnings determination', *American Sociological Review* 43, pp. 704–20.

BECKER, H. S. (1970) *Sociological Work: Method and Substance* (Chicago: Allen Lane).

BEECHEY, V. (1978) 'Women and production: A critical analysis of some sociological theories of women's work' in A. Kuhn and A. M. Wolpe (eds).

BEECHEY, V. (1983) and T. PERKINS, 'Women's part-time employment in Coventry: A study in the sexual division of labour' (Report submitted to the Joint EOC/SSRC Panel).

BELLER, A. (1982) 'Occupational segregation by sex: determinants and changes' in *Journal of Human Resources*, Vol. XVII, no. 3, pp. 371–92.

BELLER, A. (1982a) 'Trends in occupational segregation by sex', Working Papers in Population Studies No PS 8203, School of Social Sciences, University of Illinois at Urbana-Champaign.

BIBB, R. and W. H. FORM (1977) 'The effects of industrial occupational and sex stratification on wages in blue-collar markets' in *Social Forces*, 55, pp. 974–96.

BLACKABY, F. (1978) (ed.) *De-industrialisation* (London: Heinemann/ National Institute of Economic and Social Research).

BLACKBURN, R. M. and M. MANN (1979) *The Working Class in the Labour Market* (London: Macmillan).

BLAU, F. (1975) 'Sex segregation of workers by enterprise in clerical occupations' in Edwards, Reich and Gordon (eds).

BLAU, P. M. and O. D. DUNCAN (1967) *The American Occupational Structure* (New York: John Wiley and Sons Inc.).

BOWLES, S. and H. GINTIS (1975) 'The problem with human capital theory – A Marxian critique', in *American Economic Review* (Papers and Proceedings, May).

BOWLES, S. and H. GINTIS (1976) *Schooling in Capitalist America* (London: Routledge & Kegan Paul).

BRITTEN, N. and A. HEATH (1983) 'Women, men and social class' in E. Gamarnikow *et al. Gender, Class and Work* (London: Heinemann).

BROWN, R. (1983) 'Work histories and labour market segmentation', Paper given at the SSRC Symposium on Work History Analysis, University of Surrey, Sept. unpublished.

BRUEGEL, I. (1979) 'Women as a reserve army: a note on recent British experience, *Feminist Review* 3.

CAPLOW, T. (1954) *The Sociology of Work* (New York: McGraw-Hill).

CARCHEDI, G. (1975) 'On the economic identification of the New Middle Class', *Economy and Society*, 4(1).

CARCHEDI, G. (1977) *On the Economic Identification of Social Classes* (London: Routledge & Kegan Paul).

CAVENDISH, R. (1982) *Women on the line* (London: Routledge & Kegan Paul).

CHANEY, J. (1981) *Social networks and job information: the situation of women who return to work* (Manchester: Equal Opportunities Commission).

CHIPLIN, B. and P. J. SLOANE (1974) 'Sexual discrimination in the labour market', *British Journal of Industrial Relations*, Nov.

CHIPLIN, B. and P. J. SLOANE (1982) *Tackling Discrimination at the Work Place: An Analysis of Sex Discrimination in Britain* (Cambridge University Press).

CLARKE, L. (1980) *Occupational Choice: A Critical Review of Research in the United Kingdom* Department of Employment, Careers Services Branch, (London: HMSO).

CLARKE, L. (1980a) *The Transition from School to Work: A Critical Review of Research in the United Kingdom* Department of Employment, Careers Service Branch (London: HMSO).

COCKBURN, C. (1985) 'The gender of the job: work place relations and the reproduction of sex segregation', Paper given to ESRC Symposium on Segregation in Employment, University of Lancaster, July, unpublished.

CORCORAN, M. E. and G. H. DUNCAN (1979) 'Work history, labor force attachment, and earnings differences between races and sexes', *Journal of Human Resources*, vol. XIV, no. 1, pp. 1–20.

COYLE, A. (1982) 'Sex and skill in the organisation of the clothing industry' in J. West (ed) pp. 10–26.

COYLE, A (1984) *Redundant Women* (London: The Women's Press).

CRAIG, C., J. RUBERY, R. TARLING and F. WILKINSON (1982) *Labour market structure, industrial organisation and low pay* (Cambridge University Press).

CRAIG, C. and F. WILKINSON (1985) *Pay and Employment in Four Retail Trades*, Department of Employment Research Paper No 51 (London: HMSO).

CROMPTON, R., G. JONES and S. REID, 'Contemporary clerical work: A case study of local government' in J. West (ed.) (1982) *Work, Women and the Labour Market* (London: Routledge & Kegan Paul).

CROMPTON, R. and K. SANDERSON (1985) 'Credentials and careers',

Paper given to ESRC Symposium on Segregation in Employment at the University of Lancaster, July, unpublished.

DALE, A. and N. GILBERT (1984) 'Labour market structure in the UK: a consideration of some theories of segmentation' (unpublished paper, mimeo).

DEX, S. (1982) *Black and White School Leavers Employment: the first five years of work* Department of Employment Research Paper No. 33 (London: HMSO).

DEX, S. (1984) *Women's Work Histories: an analysis of the Women and Employment Survey*, Department of Employment, Research Paper No 46 (London: HMSO).

DEX, S. (1984a) 'Work histories, women and large-scale data', *Sociological Review*, vol. 32, no. 4, pp. 637–61.

DEX, S. (1985) *The Sexual Division of Work: Conceptual Revolutions in the Social Sciences* (Brighton: Wheatsheaf).

DEX, S. and L. SHAW (1986) *British and American Women at Work: Do Equal Opportunities Policies Matter?* (London: Macmillan).

DEX, S. and S. PERRY (1984) 'Women's employment changes in the 1970s', *Employment Gazette*, vol. 92, no. 4, pp. 151–64.

DOERINGER, P. B. and M. J. PIORE (1971) *Internal Labor Markets and Manpower analysis,* (Lexington, Massachusetts: D. C. Heath & Co).

DOERINGER, P. B. and N. BOSANQUET (1973) 'Is there a dual labour market in Great Britain?', *Economic Journal*, June.

EDWARDS, R. C., M. REICH and D. M. GORDON (eds) (1975) *Labour Market Segmentation* (Lexington, Massachusetts & Lexington, Books: D. C. Heath & Co).

ELIAS, P. (1983) 'Occupational mobility and part time work (Institute for Employment Research, University of Warwick mimeo).

ELIAS, P. and B. MAIN (1982) *Women's working lives: Evidence from the National Training Survey* (Institute for Employment Research, University of Warwick).

ENGLAND, P. (1982) 'The failure of human capital theory to explain occupational sex segregation', *Journal of Human Resources*, vol. XVII, no. 3, pp. 358–70.

EQUAL OPPORTUNITIES COMMISSION, *Eighth Annual Report 1983*, Equal Opportunities Commission, (Manchester: HMSO 1984).

FELMLEE, D. H. (1982) 'Women's job mobility, processes within and between employers', *American Sociological Review*, vol. 47, pp. 142–51.

FELMLEE, D. H. (1984) 'Affirmative action: good, bad, or irrelevant', in *New Perspectives*, 16, US Commission on Civil Rights: Fall, pp. 23–37.

FREEMAN, C. (1982) 'The "understanding" employer' in J. West (ed.)

GERSHUNY, J. (1978) *After industrial society? The emerging self-service economy* (London: Macmillan).

GERSHUNY, J. (1983) *Social Innovation and the Division of Labour* (Oxford University Press).

GIDDENS, A. (1973) *The Class Structure of Advanced Societies* (London: Hutchinson).

GIDDENS, A. and G. MacKENZIE (1982) *Social Class and the Division of labour: essays in honour of I. Neustadt* (Cambridge University Press).

GINZBERG, G. E., et. al. (1951) Occupational Choice (New York: Columbia University Press.)

GOLDTHORPE, J. H., C. LLEWELLYN and C. PAYNE (1980) Social Mobility and Class Structure in Modern Britain (Oxford: Clarendon Press).

GOLDTHORPE, J. H. (1983) 'Women and class analysis: in defence of the conventional view', Sociology 17, pp. 465–488.

GOLDTHORPE, J. H. (1984) 'Women and class analysis: a reply to the replies', Sociology, vol. 18, no. 4, pp. 491–99.

GRANDJEAN, B. D. (1981) 'History and career in a bureaucratic labor market', American Journal of Sociology, 86, no. 5, pp. 1057–92.

HAKIM, C. (1979) Occupational Segregation, Department of Employment Research Paper No. 9 (London: HMSO).

HAKIM, C. (1981) 'Job segregation: trends in the 1970s', Employment Gazette, pp. 521–29, (Dec).

HEARN, J. (1977) 'Towards a concept of non-career', Sociological Review, 25, no. 2, pp. 273–88.

HEARN, J. (1981) 'Crisis, taboos and careers guidance', British Journal of Guidance and Counselling, vol. 9, no, 1, pp. 12–23.

HEATH, A. and N. BRITTEN (1984) 'Women's jobs do make a difference: a reply to Goldthorpe', Sociology, vol. 18, no. 4, pp. 475–90.

HUGHES, E. C. (1937) 'Institutional office and the person', American Journal of Sociology 43, pp. 404–413.

JOSEPH, G. (1983) Women at Work: the British experience (Oxford: Philip Allan).

JOSHI, H. E. (1984) Women's participation in paid work: Further analysis of the women and employment survey, Department of Employment, Research Paper No 45 (London: HMSO).

JOSHI, H. E. (1985) 'Gender inequality in the labour market and the domestic division of labour', Cambridge Journal of Economics, forthcoming.

JUSENIUS, C. L. (1976) 'The influence of work experience and typicality of occupational segregation on women's earnings', Dual Careers, vol. 4, (Washington, DC: US Department of Labor, Employment and Training Administration monograph No 21).

KILLINGSWORTH, M. (1983) Labour Supply (Cambridge University Press).

KUHN, A. and A. WOLPE (eds) (1979) Feminism and Materialism (London: Routledge & Kegan Paul).

LAWSON, T. (1981) 'Paternalism and the labour market segmentation theory' in F. Wilkinson (ed.)

LEONARD, D. and C. DELPHY (1984) 'Class analysis, gender analysis and the family', paper presented to ESRC Symposium on Gender and Stratification, University of East Anglia, (July).

LLEWELLYN, C. (1981) 'Occupational mobility and the use of the comparative method' in H. Roberts (ed.) Doing Feminist Research (London: Routledge & Kegan Paul).

LOVATT, D. and B. HAM (1984) 'The distributional implications of de-industrialisation', British Journal of Sociology, vol. XXXV, no. 4, pp. 498–521.

LOVERIDGE, R. and A. MOK (1979) Theories of Labour Market

Segmentation (The Hague: Martinus Nijhoff).

MacKENZIE, G. (1982) 'Class boundaries and the labour process' in A. Giddens and G. MacKenzie (eds).

McNALLY, F. (1979) *Women for Hire* (London: Macmillan).

McRAE, S. (1986) *Cross-class Families: a study of wives' occupational superiority*, forthcoming (Oxford University Press).

McROBBIE, A. (1978) 'Working class girls and the culture of femininity' in Women's Studies Group (ed.) *Women Take Issue* (London: Hutchinson).

McROBBIE, A. and J. GARBER (1975) 'Girls and subcultures' in *Working Papers in Cultural Studies* 7/8.

MALLIER, A. and M. ROSSER (1980) 'Part time workers and the economy', *International Journal of Manpower* 1(3).

MARTIN, J. and C. ROBERTS (1984) *Women and Employment: a lifetime perspective*, DE/OPCS, (London: HMSO).

OAKLEY, A. (1974) *The sociology of housework* (Oxford: Martin Robertson)

OAKLEY, A. (1979) *From here to maternity: becoming a mother* (Harmondsworth: Penguin Books).

PARKIN, F. (1971) *Class Inequality and Political Order* (London: MacGibbon & Kee).

PERRY, S. (1986) 'Women, part-time work and the *Women and Employment Survey*, unpublished Ph.D., University of Keele.

PINDYCK, R. S. and D. L. RUBINFELD (1976) *Econometric Models and Economic Forecasts* (London: McGraw-Hill).

PIORE, M. J. (1975) 'Notes for a theory of labour market stratification' in Edwards, Reich and Gordon (eds).

POLLERT, A. (1981) *Girls, Wives, Factory Lives* (London: Macmillan).

POULANTZAS, N. (1973) 'On social classes', *New Left Review*, 78, pp. 27–50.

POWER, M. (1983) 'From home production to wage labour: women as a reserve army of labor', *Review of Radical Political Economics*, XV, no. 1, pp. 71–91.

PURCELL, K. (1979) 'Militancy and acquiescence amongst women workers' in S. Burman (ed.) *Fit Work for Women* (London: Croom Helm).

ROBERTS, K. (1968) 'The entry into employment: an approach towards a general theory', *Sociological Review*, 16, pp. 165–84.

ROBERTS, K. (1973) 'An alternative theory of occupational choice', *Education and Training*, 15, pp. 310–11.

ROBINSON, O. and J. WALLACE (1984) *Part-time Employment and Sex Discrimination Legislation in Great Britain* Department of Employment Research Paper No. 43, (London: HMSO).

ROSENFELD, R. (1979) 'Women's occupational careers: individual and structural explanations', *Sociology of Work and Occupations*, vol. 6, no. 3, pp. 283–311.

ROSENFELD, R. (1980) 'Race and sex differences in career dynamics', *American Sociological Review*, 45, 4, pp. 583–609.

RUBERY, J. (1978) 'Structured labour markets, worker organization and low pay', *Cambridge Journal of Economics*, 2.1, pp. 17–36.

RUBERY, J. and F. WILKINSON (1979) 'Notes on the nature of the labour process in the secondary sector' in *Low Pay and Labour Markets Segmentation* (Conference papers, Cambridge).

RUBERY, J. and R. J. TARLING (1983) 'Women in the recession', Economic Reprint No. 68 (Department of Applied Economics, University of Cambridge).

RYAN, P. (1981) 'Segmentation, duality and the internal labour market', in F. Wilkinson (ed.).

SANDELL, S. H. and SHAPIRO, D. (1978) 'The theory of human capital and the earnings of women: a reexamination of the evidence', *Journal of Human Resources*, 13, pp. 103–117.

SHAW, L. B. (1983) *Unplanned Careers: the working lives of middle-aged women*, (Massachusetts: D. C. Heath and Co.).

SHAW, L. B. (1983a) 'Does working part time contribute to women's occupational segregation?', Paper presented to annual meeting of the Mid-West Economics Association, St Louis, Missouri, mimeo, (April).

SHERRATT, N. (1983) 'Girls, jobs and glamour', *Feminist Review*, 15, pp. 47–61.

SILVERSTONE, R. (1974) 'The office secretary' (unpublished Ph.D. thesis, City University, London).

SILVERSTONE, R. (1975) 'Just a Sec?', *Personnel Management*, vol. 7, no. 6 (June).

SLEEPER, R. A. (1975) 'Industrial mobility and the life cycle', *British Journal of Industrial Relations*.

SLOCUM, W. L. (1966) *Occupational Careers: a sociological perspective*, (Chicago: Aldine).

SMITH, R. (1976) 'Sex and occupational role on Fleet Street' in D. L. Barker and S. Allen (eds) *Dependence and Exploitation in Work and Marriage* (New York: Longman).

SORENSEN, A. B. (1983) 'Sociological research on the labor market', *Work and Occupations*, vol. 10, no. 3, pp. 261–287.

SORENSEN, A. B. (1983) 'Women's employment patterns after marriage', *Journal of Marriage and the Family*, May, pp. 311–21.

SORENSEN, A. B. (1983a) 'Children and their mothers', *Social Science Research*, 12, pp. 26–43.

SPILERMAN, S. (1977) 'Careers, labor market structures and socio-economic achievement', *American Journal of Sociology* 83, pp. 551–93.

STANWORTH, M. (1984) 'Women and class analysis: A reply to John Goldthorpe', *Sociology*, vol. 18, no. 2, pp. 159–70.

STEWART, A., K. PRANDY and R. M. BLACKBURN (1980) *Social Stratification and Occupations* (London: Macmillan).

STEWART, M. and C. A. GREENHALGH (1982) 'The training and experience dividend', *Employment Gazette*, August, pp. 329–340.

STEWART, M. and C. A. GREENHALGH (1984) 'Work history patterns and occupational attainment of women', *Economic Journal*, 94, no. 375, pp. 493–519.

SUPER, D. E. (1953) 'A theory of vocational development', *American Psychologist* 8, pp. 185–90.

TERKEL, S. (1974) *Working* (Harmondsworth: Penguin 1975 edition).

THATCHER, A. R. (1978) 'Labour supply and employment trends' in Blackaby, F.

THEODORE, A. (ed.) (1971) *The Professional Woman* (Cambridge, Massachusetts: Schenkman).

TUMA, N. B. and M. T. HANNAN (1976) 'Approaches to the censoring problem in analysis of event histories' in Schuessler, K. F. (ed.) *Sociological Methodology* (San Francisco: Jossey Barr).

WAJCMAN, J. (1983) *Women in Control* (Milton Keynes: The Open University Press).

WALBY, S. (1984) 'Gender, class and stratification: towards a new approach', Paper given at ESRC Symposium on Gender and Stratification, University of East Anglia (July).

WALBY, S. (1985) 'Segregation in employment in social and economic theory', Paper given to ESRC Symposium on Segregation in Employment, University of Lancaster, July, unpublished.

WEST, J. (1978) 'Women, sex, and class' in A. Kuhn and A. Wolpe (eds), *Feminism and Materialism* (London: Routledge & Kegan Paul).

WEST, J. (ed.) (1982) *Work, Women and the Labour Market* (London: Routledge & Kegan Paul).

WILLIS, P. E. (1977) *Learning to Labour: how working class kids get working class jobs* (Farnborough: Saxon House).

WILKINSON, F. (ed.) (1981) *The Dynamics of Labour Market Segmentation* (London: Academic Press).

WOODWARD, J. (1960) *The Saleswoman: a study of attitudes and behaviour in retail distribution* (London: Pitman).

WRIGHT, E. O. (1978) *Class, Crisis and the State* (London: New Left Books).

YEANDLE, S. (1984) *Women's Working Lives: patterns and strategies* (London: Tavistock Publications).

Index

DATE DUE